Woman Worship 4

Dean Jéan-Pierre

CalmWaters Entertainment Group, Inc. presents

Woman Worship 4

Dean Jéan-Pierre

CalmWaters Entertainment Group, Inc.

Library of Congress Cataloging-in-Publication Data
Dean Jéan-Pierre
ISBN: 978-0-692-37566-2

WOMAN WORSHIP 4
© 2018 by Dean Jéan-Pierre
CalmWaters Entertainment Group, Inc.
www.calmwatersentertainment.com

Dean Jéan-Pierre
www.deanjeanpierre.com

Book Design: Cynthia Colbert
Photographer: Alana Stewart

Dean Jéan-Pierre

Table o f Contents

Stay 13
Indifference.. 14
Melancholy 15
Glance 16
Anniversary 17
Fire 18
Violins 19
Intimate... 20
Grateful... 21
Façade 22
A million Kisses.. 23
Lost.. 24
He Will Appreciate You... 25
This Time 26
Man & Wife 27
Taste.. 28
I Surrender 29
Wonderful 30
Weightless 31
On That Day... 32
Conviction... 33
Thank You, My Friend.. 34
So It Goes 35
Greener Grass... 36
Sanity... 37
Man Up... 38
Say What You Have To Say 39
Adult Love 40
Loveless Marriage... 41
The Woman of the House... 42
If You Knew How Much I Miss You............................. 43
Melancholy Days Like This 44
Single Woman... 45
One Last Time... 46
John Denver Laments 47
Your Skin... 48
Give Me 49
This Is Your Life... 50

When He Is Ready 51
Thank You For Caring 52
Soft Kisser 53
Greatness 54
Alternate Universe 55
Ugly Madness 56
Fleeting 57
Safe 58
The Other Fairytale 59
A Pain That Never Goes Away 60
As Surely 61
Journey 62
My Secret 63
Your Smile 64
Pleasure is Coming 65
First Kiss 66
The Dreamer 67
Inarticulate 68
Soft Words 69
Spiraling 70
Until You Were Gone 71
Catch My Breath 73
Held 74
Your Words 75
Invisible 76
You Promised 77
Neverending 78
Profound 79
My Body Aches 80
Fading into Obscurity 81
Insecure 82
Something about You 84
There Are Moments 85
More than Good Enough 86
Every Woman 87
Illusions 88
Dream Not Deferred 89
Tell Me 90
The Weekend 91
Dysfunctional Marriage 92
The Edge of Insanity 93

Awakened 94
Breakfast Smells Good.. 95
Life's Compromise.. 96
She Needs... 97
The Silence of Your Thoughts.................................. 98
Happy Emptiness.. 99
Sweet Words 100
Nostalgia.. 101
Sweet Innocence 102
Mid-Life Crisis... 103
Fatigue 104
When.. 105
Ugly Heart 106
A New You 107
Passing Time... 108
Crying Orgasms.. 109
Defenseless 110
Solitude 111
Take Care of Yourself 112
Tired 113
Ain't It Funny 114
Come Here... 115
Amazing Lover 116
Contagious 117
Take Me to Church.. 118
Bow 119
Children 120
For The Briefest Moment....................................... 121
Almost Spiritual... 122
Held.. 123
Happiness.. 124
Struggle 125
Grace.. 126
Stay Still 127
Shiver 128
Full.. 129
Whisper Softly 130
The Best Woman 131
You.. 132
Silence 133
Life Happens 134

Sleeper 135
Your Lips 136
Serena 137
Deserve 138
Not Good Enough 139
You Love Me 140
Sweet Soca 141
Just For Him 142
Something Special 143
A Mother Knows 144
The Beautiful Struggle 145
Soul Energy 146
Clouds 147
Something So Beautiful 148
Eternity 149
Freedom 150
Sleepless 151
Moments 152
Tremors 153
Jealousy 154
I'm Not Ready 155
Urgency 156
Promises 157
Three Words 158
You Don't Say My Name Anymore 159
Black Girl Magic 160

Poetry captures and keeps our memories safe. It touches that secret place in our souls, where hopes, dreams and love always remain possible. It is our sanctuary from the world where we allow ourselves permission to feel life without judgment. It is that window into our soul where we strip away the façade of the world and swim in the beauty of words. Poetry lets words speak to you as if you are having an internal, intimate conversation. Woman Worship 4 is that conversation with yourself you should have over a glass of wine. Lose yourself in the beauty of this collection. You deserve it.

www.deanjeanpierre.com

Dedicated to my Aunty Talin. She loved me like a King. Loved me so much, it still brings tears to my eyes. She loved me like a mother loves a child. In many ways, she was. I hope she knew how much I loved her in this life. And if she didn't, I hope to tell her just how much in the Afterlife. In the meantime, I tell her how much I love her in my dreams.

Stay

Let us stay in bed this morning
It is much too cold outside for lovers
We can pretend the world does not exist
We have everything we need right here
While everyone is busy working
Doing the things needed to get ahead in life
All I want to do is feel your naked body against mine
Taste your lips as we kiss
Inhale your breath as we give each other life
I want to hear about your dreams
I want to feel the smile on your face warming my hands
There are things about you that are still unspoken
Things about me I want to share with only you
We have a history that is in the past
The ghosts of past hurts still keep us company
It speaks to us in the silence of our conversations
I want to bury mine six feet under
So we can move forward with our future
Stay with me under the covers
While everyone is busy working
Let us become more than just lovers.

10-21-13...8:58 am
Listening to Lifetime by Maxwell

Indifference

She loves him more than she cares to admit to herself
Loving him leaves her vulnerable to being hurt again
A piece of her soul still wanders the universe lost in search of answers
God has gone quiet when she prays in the evenings
She only has faith now in the coldness of indifference
Falling in love is a temporary high
Heartbreak eventually takes its rightful place in her heart
It is an expected conclusion once it becomes part of your psyche
How she wishes for the innocence of her youth
When every motive was not met with suspicion
In his eyes she feels his love
In his kisses they feel like forever
But she knows that forever is moment by moment
She wants to trust what her heart is saying
But her heart is blind and easily misled
So she pretends to be indifferent
All she wants is to be held by the man she loves
And to know when he holds her his heart is hers.

11-3-13...11:23am
Listening to Fire & Rain by James Taylor

Melancholy

Melancholy washes over my soul in waves until I drown
There are days when my life is too heavy a burden to carry
Even though I am blessed I feel unworthy
A sad love song plays in my head
I wonder where all the time has went
Have I done my best with the time God has given me
Have I squandered too many opportunities
Is there still time to make amends
I wonder if all the bad I have done
Will my good deeds even matter when judgment day comes
The central theme of my life has always been to be the good daughter
The one that makes everyone proud
The burden of expectations keeps me fearful
My best will never be good enough
It fuels my creativity in search of places never traveled
But with each success comes this empty feeling I am not good enough
Self-doubt eats me up inside
I am once again that little girl without any confidence
So shy I would hide for hours in my room when there was company
Melancholy sweeps over me seducing me in her arms
It feels like I am home again in my room
I can shed my tears alone in quiet
I am understood when I bear my soul
Melancholy never turns me away
She loves me for who I am
Every day her kisses grow sweeter
Her whispers become more insistent
Asking me to love her, to choose her over everyone else
I have felt love so deep it has brought me to tears
It left me devastated for years to come
Melancholy has promised me a life of eternal peace
Take my hand she smiles and come with me.

11-4-13...3:51pm
Listening to Strange Way by Firefall

Glance

A knowing glance between women
They know they share similar stories
A quiet legacy passed down through the years
It is a language of shared tears
Sprinkled with moments of surreal joy
And there is always unspeakable grief that no human being should ever feel
Somehow they persevere because embodied in their legacy
Is an unwavering belief in who they are as women
Sometimes they lose themselves forgetting who they are
Their strength becomes a temporary weakness
In that glance is a resolve to always rise and never succumb
The innocent eyes of children are always watching
Tomorrow arrives with new surprises
A gift that their faith has been rewarded.

11-5-13...8:51 am
Listening to Missing You by John Waite

Anniversary

Good morning my love
Today is a blessed day filled with joy
The years we have shared
The times we have spent mean so much to me
Lucky is not a word I usually entertain
But in a world of such uncertainty
I am blessed and lucky the powers of the universe sent me your love
No relationship is ever perfect
I have failed you more than once
I am certain I will again
In all our trials and tribulations love was a fire in my heart
The breath in my soul
The rock which remained unbroken
I will fight for us because without you I have nothing
You are everything to me
Without your love as my light
My world would forever live in darkness
If I haven't said it already this morning happy anniversary
You are the joy of my soul
The happiness of my existence
And I thank you for loving me something beautiful

11-6-13...8:29 am
Listening to Free Fallin' by Tom Petty

Fire

Fire burns in your skin
Hot enough to start a fireplace
Heat tastes so good on your lips
Feed me your passion one kiss at a time
I want to savor every morsel as I swallow your strength
A surge of desire envelops my thoughts
Nothing makes sense when you kiss me like this
If you are to be my ruin in this moment
I would not have the strength to stop my own demise
I am ashes in your hands scattering in the wind
If you are to be my salvation please save me now
I am unable to continue like this without ananchor
My feelings for you are too deep to ignore
They are simmering below the surface
Hidden behind my many denials
Each lie turns to truth when we kiss
This is what I have been praying for all my life
I want to embrace this love with an open heart
I want the fire in my soul to rise to the surface
Take flight into a love forever beautiful.

11-12-13...8:10 pm
Listening to If You Think You're Lonely Now by Bobby Womack
(KC of Jodeci's remake is pretty good too)

Violins

The music plays softly in my head
I want to dance with you under the moonlight
You are my only captive audience
My life is out of step with how I feel
My feet have no rhythm
All this beautiful music should be heard
Two hearts loving in unison
Play the violin in my heart
Listen to my sappy love song
Close your eyes listen to my soul sing
Heart wrenching melodies wrought with love
Lyrics evoking my dreams for us
A life filled with love and laughter
The dawn is fast approaching
The moon fades away to welcome the sunrise
The music in my heart is my constantcompanion
It plays for only you to hear.

11-14-13...10am
Listening to I'm Wishing on a Star by Rose Royce

Intimate

Quiet thoughts of you arouse
My eyes close to hold you captive in my mind
We are intimate without being physical
You know what pleases me without a word being spoken
Come closer I need to taste your scent on my lips
Feel the warmth of life in your breasts
A slow tremble moves through my body
An explosion of passion looms on the horizon
Your smile gives me permission to ravish you to my heart's content
The evening is young and filled with a lover's promise
A promise to seduce the soul and steal its breath away
I want to take my time to linger and enjoy your secrets
While we forget time exists and make love beyond eternity.

11-20-13...4:03pm
Listening to Sail On by The Commodores

Grateful

You never really needed me
In time I thought you would at least want me
I made it too easy by giving you everything
Without ever asking for anything in return
You took it like a thief without a conscience
You stole my heart with a smile on your face
You ravished my body with sweet lies of commitment
You cannot change the nature of a man's heart
No matter how deeply you love him
No matter how sweet the loving
It's hard watching you walk away
You never once looked back to say a kind word
Maybe that was for the best
There is nothing worse for a woman's heart than false hope
You were an addiction I could not kick
Even now just the thought of you makes my body react to a memory
You did me a favor by being who you are
A man with no loyalties
A thief without a soul
A man without a conscience
You gave me back myself when you left
For that, I thank you.

1-22-14...10:12am
Listening to Let It Breathe by Water Liars

Facade

A deep well of sadness resides in my soul
My shadow has held me captive for so many years
My past will not let me move forward
Dreams lay at my feet in decay
The stench of broken promises sometimes too much to bear
Who am I now if my word has no meaning
If my passion is empty of emotion
I am just sailing by on the promise of what once could have been
The face in the mirror turns away from my stare
Who am I now if I don't have myself to believe in
I crave to be happy but my sadness remains hungry
I see myself in the eyes of strangers
Struggling to understand who I have become
The answers remain silent
The questions will not be quiet
From the moment I wake up life is a puzzle I am trying to solve
My days are spent going down rabbit holes
Each day feels like Groundhog Day
It all seems pointless the ship has gotten lost
The sun forgets to shine
Evening is my ray of light
It is when I feel like myself
As if I can finally exhale and take off the mask
There is no one to see me when I am just me.

11-21-13...11:30am
Listening to If You're Gone by Matchbox Twenty

A Million Kisses

If you leave me with nothing else
Leave me with the feel of your lips upon my skin
Touch me lovingly with your hands and fingers
So my body will always remember you were here
Whisper soft words of pleasure in my ears
So my mind can recollect your voice when I fall asleep
Kiss me everywhere you please
My body is a canvas waiting for your lips to kiss
A million delicious kisses plus one more plus one more
I am always so greedy for your taste
It is not my fault I am addicted to your kisses
They soothe my spirit much in the way wine makes me mellow
If it were not for my pride I would beg you to stay and never leave
I would tell you all the things your kisses do to me
I would tell you I imagine your lips far more often than I would like to
admit
Something tells you already know all of this
The way you kiss me there are no secrets my lips can ever keep.

3-22-14...8:43 evening
Listening to Losing My Religion by R.E.M.

Lost

I feel lost, unable to find my way back to myself
When did I take the wrong fork in the road
Who are these people claiming to be my friends
With all their beautiful smiles and empty promises
Feeding me lies because it's what I want to hear
Criticism only feeds my issues of feeling unworthy
The truth won't set me free
It will drag me back to the reality from which I cannot escape
Everywhere is littered with broken dreams
Of lives and things of what could have been
I want to bend my knees and pray
But will he even remember my voice
I have been gone for so long now
At the end of the road I see a light not visible to most
It flickers like a beacon, a star
There has to be something better ahead
There has to be more than just this
And then I remember what I should not have forgotten
Even in the wilderness there is shelter
Even in doubt there is hope
Even when you are lost you are never alone
The light shines ahead
My heart is open to what the future brings

3-26-14…9:08 in the morning
Listening to Name by The Goo Goo Dolls

He Will Appreciate You

He will appreciate when you are gone
He will claim to be a changed man, please come back home
Where was this love for all those years
Where was the man you married for better or worse
Where was the man who turned his back while you cried in pain
You have given your life to his care
Fed him like the King you thought he was
Born him beautiful children to carry on his name
No matter what you did it was never good enough
For so many years you felt invisible in his presence
He ridiculed you in front of family and friends
Your happiness did not even matter
You were treated worse than the help
He expected you to carry on with a smile
Be thankful for a roof over your head
His idea of affection was telling you he wants some this evening
No romance to tease your senses
No words to make you feel special like a lady
You were expected to lay there and perform for his pleasure
You felt worse than a lady of the night
Even they are paid for their services
There comes a point when you will reach your limit
It will not matter if you are not ready to leave
It will not matter all the material things you will leave behind
Because happiness cannot find you unless you find yourself
You cannot cower and ask for strength
You cannot want better and stay in your place
Your place has to be created by you
You have to step out on faith and embrace your inner Goddess
It is in the DNA of all women because God placed it there
When you are ready to leave
Nothing on this earth can hold you back
From the life you were meant to live.

4-6-14…11:04 in the morning
Listening to Pieces of Me by Ledisi

This Time

Maybe this time someone will love you because you were his choice
They will see all the beauty in you that has gone unappreciated for so long
This time you won't feel as if you are begging for love
This time you will be seen for who you are and not what you can give
All along you said it didn't matter
You were content to receive any kind of attention
But deep down it ate at your spirit
Dragging you into the darkness
Silently destroying your self-confidence
And when you least expected something good to happen
Someone saw through the facade of a woman lost
A hand was given
Respect was shown
The woman dying in the darkness
Rose into the light to illuminate her spirit
And here you are now being all that you should have always been
Your destiny was waiting for you to find your strength
To claim the life you were meant to live.

11.3.14...6:16 in the evening on the train
Listening to These Are Days by 10,000 Maniacs

Man & Wife

It has been so long since I held you in my arms
I never forgot your scent, how you felt when we made love
You would sigh whenever I held you close
As if you were letting go all the troubles of the world
How I wish we had been able to swim through the storm
Find our way to shore and hold on until we were safe
Stubborn we were, no one wanting to admit theirmistakes
We both played a hand in burying ourrelationship
Instead we let a good thing go and now all we have are memories
So many regrets we cannot take back
So many hurtful words I still remember
So many nights we went to bed so damn angry
Maybe time will allow us to have some perspective
Maybe it will help us to remember why we fell in love
Even if we can never be together as man and wife
Maybe one day if we find ourselves in the same place
We can sit down and have a civilconversation
Maybe you will laugh at something funny I might say
Maybe your smile will make the past easier to reconcile
Before we both know it, hours will have passed as we enjoy each
other's company.

11.4.14…11:17 in the morning
Listening to Collide by Howie Day

Taste

Fingers grazing your skin
You purr ever so softly
Heat rises like mist from your flesh
Warming my fingertips with your arousal
The taste of you on my lips,
Releases a guttural moan that wakes the evening.
Even the night cannot sleep when we make love with abandon.

11.21.14...8:41pm
Listening to Pretty Wings by Maxwell

I Surrender

Today I surrender because I don't have the answers
My faith has been misplaced in false friends
They have used my kindness and turned it into a sword
Along the way killing my dreams while building their own
Today I surrender because I am tired
My dreams have turned to ashes
The Phoenix has lost it wings
The things I placed value on are meaningless
They have not brought me the desired comfort from hardship
I am still walking in darkness even though my eyes are wideopen
I am ready to listen
I am ready to humble my expectations
Maybe then I will see beyond my ego
Allow my heart to lead instead of my selfish needs
Today I surrender because it is the only way to find myself.

1.12.15....10:19 in the morning
Listening to Wherever You Will Go by TheCalling

Wonderful

Your lips feel wonderful on me
They make me sigh with content
There is a deep hunger in you that I need to taste
It is a craving that needs to be fed
Please don't think I only want you in the physical sense
What I am feeling right now could only be satisfied by kissing your skin
Words would leave me unsatisfied right now
They cannot soothe this hunger to taste you naked
To drink from the deep stream flowing through your valley
To hear the fury of your passion as you praise your god multiple times
The voice of your pleasure feeds my desire to please
It is a gift you give to me without truly knowing how much it means
You are wonderful in so many ways my words cannot fully express
Listen to them silent on my tongue
When I kiss you and taste the fire buried in your skin
If you knew how wonderful you felt
You would never want me to ever stop
Not even for a breath because being in love like this
Is the treasure everyone hopes to find
The dream everyone silently prays for every night they go to sleep.

1.19.15...7:51 on the train
Listening to Let's Stay Together by Al Green

Weightless

Making love to you defies definition
It is an experience that leaves me searching for words and answers
Metaphors cannot fully capture the depth of our passion
It is a dance with its own rhythm
A painting so amazing
A poem flowing with life
A song sung only for us
Your touch leaves me in a constant daze
The day is a dream when I am awake
You have exceeded all expectations
You are a memory I can summon at any given moment
You were a fantasy that became a beautiful reality
I now wake up with every morning.

11.21.14...8:22 morning
Listening to Loving You by Minnie Riperton

On That Day

On that day when you close your eyes
You feel the presence of God calling you home
You want to say that you did what you loved
You followed your heart even when it was broken
You fell in love and it hurt like hell
You fell again but this time your faith was rewarded
You took a chance when everyone told you to play it safe
On that day when you close your eyes
Your biggest sin will be that of regret
You allowed others to dictate your path
You allowed your passion to be compromised
There were too many obstacles you might say
Dreams are not realized overnight
The hard work comes when no one is applauding
You are your own sold out audience
This is when you find out how much you really want it
Is it something burning in your gut
Is it something you can live without
Does it haunt your every waking hour
On that day when you close your eyes
I pray there is a smile in your heart.

12.10.14...7:56 on the morning train
Listening to Easy Like Sunday Morning by The Commodores

Conviction

There are words she says with so much conviction
She is living them for the first time in her life
Embracing what others have taken for granted
There is an urgency in her tone, as if she is in on some secret
Love can do that to you
Bringing the universe so close you can reach out and feel life
It feels like you are in conversation with God
A love like that taps into all your senses
Even when you are fast sleep
You are consumed with the fire of arousal.

12.10.14...8:08 am
Listening to Heaven's Here on Earth by Tracy Chapman

Thank You, My Friend

There are days when I miss my friend so much
The weight of his loss comes down on me like a hammer
I am old enough now to understand death
How it leaves you empty and searching for answers
But with each loved one lost it still makes no sense
There were so many things left unsaid
So many conversations I needed toshare
I never thought you would die so young
I thought we would have more time,
Maybe vacation together, just talk about stuff
You know, have drinks and some laughs like good friends do
I wonder if you knew the impact you had on my life
How often I would turn to you for guidance
Our conversations rambled on for hours
We were friends, no longer just student and teacher
Six months later I still cannot grasp the silence of your voice
A phone call from you at odd hours of the night
Now I wish I had been a better friend
Somehow able to see past your facade of indifference
Always concerned about others but not yourself
I wish I had been a better friend and heard your silent call for help
There are still days when I listen to your recorded voice
So filled with life, sarcasm and good humor
As long as I live my friend
I will miss you forever
Thank you for the gift of your friendship
It has made all the difference in my life
Until the accident will.

12.19.14...5:25 in the evening
(For my friend, Mark Stephen Moross)
Listening to Time of Your Life by Green Day

So It Goes

You were here for a moment
You did beautiful things with your time given
You did not change the world
Just the lives of a few people who will be forever grateful
Your life mattered to someone
It mattered to me
You were loved by many
You were loved by me
You will be missed by all
You will be forever missed by me
Safe travels on your journey my friend
Tell Vonnegut and Salinger I said hello
Tell Holden there is good in the world
And is the catcher still trying to save all the children?
Did Billy Pilgrim ever find some peace?
In the immortal words of Vonnegut, so it goes.

12.22.14...8 in the morning
Listening to Return to Me by October Project

Greener Grass

There is a fear of being alone as we grow older
It feels like something is missing because society tells us so
Marriage and children brings us happiness
A life without that invites questions
How can it be a choice many will ask
Even as they crave the freedom you have
You want to tell them you're not unhappy
Even though there are days when you do get lonely
It's just human nature to crave the warmth of affection
I am sure they too would quietly admit
A few days away from the kids and husband would be wonderful
Some quiet time to read a book,
Maybe watch a movie or just exhale for a moment
Life gets too busy sometimes
We forget to appreciate the small blessings we have
Even if you are alone or have someone to share your life
There is much to be grateful for as you journey through your day
Because the grass is always greener on the other side.

12.23.14...8:07 on the train.
Listening to Where Are You Going by Dave Matthews Band

Sanity

I slept inside your warmth last night
Wrapped around me you held me close
Your love was our only protection and that is always enough
Murmuring incoherently we moved like soft waves seeking shelter
Our passion refused to be washed away as the night grew older
Your glow was as beautiful as the soft moonlight
Your passion as fiery as the coming sunrise
Closing my eyes even for a moment felt like a lifetime without you
I have known those endless days of despair
Knowing we would be here like this kept me sane
I am the richest man in the world tonight
My heart is filled with love
My prayers have been answered
I no longer have to dream about you my love
You are right here in my arms where you will always be.

1.14.15...8:13 on the train
Listening to Adore by Prince

Man Up

A man does not make a woman promises and breaks her heart
He does not allow her to be vulnerable and finally exhale
And then without warning brings her world crashing down
She has to get up again to face the world
Look herself in the mirror and question herchoices
She has done nothing wrong except to believe in love
She has given her all again to someone she thought had her back
No one ever said life is fair, even though it should be sometimes
A heart can only take so much
Faith can only carry you so far
Every heart has its limit
She has not reached hers as yet
She will dust her smile off, exhale again
Believing from all the boys shemeets,
A man will step forward to claim her heart

1.15.15...7:58 train
Listening to Waiting In Vain by Bob Marley

Say What You Have to Say

You don't love me anymore
Saying those words cut me to the bone
It is the truth without the smiles and promises
The laughter in your voice has gone quiet
The want in your voice is now silent
I am not the woman you want even if you cannot say so to my face
You want me to leave so you won't be the bad guy
Not this time, just tell me the truth
Say what you have to say, so I can do what I have to do
Don't worry about hurting my feelings
When you love this deeply
Getting hurt is always a possibility
A relationship cannot survive with only one person
Your clothes is still here but your heart has already left
When we make love you don't even see me
I am right here, the woman who sacrificed for our future
The one who believed in you when no else did
Your dreams are now realized
The wings I gave you to fly have taken you away from me
All I have left now are memories and what could have been
The sun will rise in the morning
I will find the strength to move past this pain
It will be hard because the love I have you is as deep as my faith
So say what you have to say, so I can do what I need to do.

1.22.15...8:06 am
Listening to Can You Stop The Rain by Peabo Bryson

Adult Love

For the first time in my adult life I feel love
Love filled with so much passion my heart is full
It scares me this feeling of completeness
What if when morning comes it disappears without a trace
Putting your faith in something you want to last forever
But knowing forever could last as long as tomorrow
Then what shall you do with all this love you saved for one person
It keeps growing inside of you with nowhere to call its home
No anchor to hold it steady
It consumes you with the fervor of an addiction
It is not a cure you seek but validation of being worthy of love
Love embraced you again this morning
You exhaled in his arms and said a prayer
The hard work is not yet over
The seed has been planted but love needs to be nurtured as it
continues to grow
Even the most beautiful flower will die before its time
If it is left alone to fend for itself.

1.29.15...8:03 in the morning
Listening to Are You The Woman by Kashif

Loveless Marriage

A man sleeps besides me but my bed is cold
My refrigerator is full but my heart is empty
There are no words of love and affection in this house
Only a voice of anger and entitlement
The voice of a man who doesn't know he is blessed with the love of a
good woman
I hear the neighbors laughing over dinner but my heart is crying
This isn't a marriage anymore, maybe it never was
Most days it feels like a funeral and it's my own death I am watching
I buried myself with false pride and low self-esteem
This person I have become I no longer recognize
What happened to the woman who would take no shit from any man
She spoke her mind without fear of reprisal
She was a champion without a belt
A woman who led while others silently followed
That woman was beaten down through the years
Left to perish because she was seen as too strong, too independent
Even an independent woman needs strong arms to hold her when she
feels weak
A strong voice to let her know when she is wrong
Every night I feel alone in this empty home
We sleep on opposite sides of the bed
My body craves affection and a kind word
Hope has left this loveless marriage
It's time I packed up my bags and my heart
Head out into the world and find what God has in store for me
I have wasted enough good years
Cried too many damn tears
It's time for the sun to shine on my face
It's time for me rise and reclaim my life.

1.29.15...8:17 am
Listening to A House Is Not A Home by Luther Vandross

The Woman of the House

The day hasn't yet begun
You are already weary of expectations
There are miles to travel before you rest your head
Sleep is a luxury you cannot afford
Being sick is out of the question
You are the engine that gets everything started
You are supposed to have all the answers
Even when you are not up for the job you soldier on
Along the way you somehow figure it out
It is what your mother did before you
It is what her mother did before her
Women are the soil of the earth
They are the sun in the sky
They are the moon lighting the way
They are the air that we breathe
Without them there is no life
Without them nothing can grow
We take for granted what should be revered
Only when it's too late do we appreciate hard work and dedication
Loyalty so fierce sometimes to their own detriment
At day's end there should be a sanctuary awaiting her presence
A place she can go by herself and exhale for a moment
Just to allow the world and her thoughts some separation
Let the woman inside rise to surface without fear of being hurt
Even the woman of the house needs some privacy
Without having to worry about the needs and wants of everybody else.

1.27.15...10:29 in the morning
Listening to Ribbons In The Sky by Stevie Wonder

If You Knew How Much I Miss You

When I begin to miss you this much
I delve into my special treasure of memories of us
There is always one that soothes my loneliness temporarily
You hold me tenderly in your arms
Brushing a wisp of hair from my face
You look so intense at times; it sweeps me away in a rush of emotions
Even after all this time my heart cannot stop beating so fast
I get excited to feel your warmth and have your attention all to myself
You graze my cheeks with your fingertips
My fire rises like a burning building
It is such a simple gesture of affection and yet so intimate
It pulls me deeper into the passion we share
It consumes me and I cannot tell where fantasy and reality ends
I cannot imagine now never having you in my life
The world would seem odd, empty without your presence
It feels sometimes that you were always there,
Quietly waiting for me to come to you
If you knew how much I miss you
You would never stay away this long
You would never go days, weeks without my kisses and my love
Being without them would cause your heart to revolt
By any means necessary you would make your way to me.

1.27.15...10:18 two hour work delay
Listening to Come Back to Me by Janet Jackson

Melancholy Days Like This

Melancholy days like this when I cannot see the dark from the light
When I am blinded by my own insecurities and dreams not yet realized
There is a weight on my heart I just cannotshake
It all merges into one consciousness leaving me reeling to find myself
So I reach for my happiest memory one that I know will console me
Every time it fades further into a place I don't recognize
I see the face of the child I once was
I see the faces of loved ones I havelost
I want to tell that child hold on to every dream of happiness
It is fleeting like rays of sunlight through your fingers
I want to tell that child tell everyone you love how you feel
Soon they will be gone too soon and the silence is eternally deafening
Memories are beautiful but cannot sustain you no matter what anyone says
Even when loved ones appear in your dreams
There is an unspoken silence of a future not lived
Of a destiny not yet fulfilled and all they have left is what could have been
Melancholy days like this I pray for rain so I can embrace the mood of
my sadness
Just for today I can feel sorry for myself and then tomorrow get back
to my life
Over a glass of good wine and a good book my mind drifts away to
another planet
The temporary blues of melancholy will soon pass
Tomorrow morning I will open my eyes and be thankful to still be here.

1.29.15...8:22 am
Listening to Orange Sky by Alexi Murdoch

Single Woman

Your makeup looks good this morning
You are dressed finer than a supermodel
You are keeping yourself in shape
Eating right and loving yourself again
You are even going to church on Sundays
You don't need a man to complete you even though society says otherwise
It would be nice to have one so you tell all your friends
They all say you're a catch and cannot understand
Why such a beautiful woman like you is still single
You don't wonder about that anymore
It takes too much energy giving thought to something you can't control
You count your blessings
You do the things you love
Waiting for a future which might never come is a waste of time
There are days when you miss the comfort of having a man around
The simple things that couples do without thinking about it
One day you would love to have that feeling
Until that day comes you will live your life to the fullest
Tomorrow's happiness is promised to no one.

1.29.15. 7:52 on the train listening to Annie's Song. John Denver

One Last Time

One last time before you leave
Hold me close and don't say a word
The moment will speak in its voice of silence
We will remember the journey and how it led us here
It was filled with many firsts, good times and in the end so much hurt
Maybe one day when I remember this moment
A wistful smile will play on my face
I will remember something special you once said
My heart will somehow manage to lessen the pain
It is what we do when we try to make sense of it all
But the future is not here and all I have is this moment
My heart is breaking and I am still a mess
I want to beg you to stay so we can figure this thing out
Too many years invested to just walk away and move on to other people
So many memories to just start all over again
Begging you to stay won't keep you here
You should never have to beg for someone's love
It should be freely given without any strings attached
Hold me just a little bit longer before you leave
It will be the last time you ever touch me like this
Maybe it's the pain speaking through my tears
I will never let another man get this close again.

1.29.15...6:16 train.
Listening to Nick Drake's Northern Sky

John Denver Laments

I think of you often more than I would like to admit sometimes
You are one of my first thoughts in the morning
You are gone but never forgotten
I hold on to the memories of our conversations
I search for clues in between your words
Trying to find your bit of happiness
Maybe it's just guilt slowly eating away at me
Even though it is a useless emotion
It cannot change the outcome of what happened
It only makes you alter your perception of what you already know
A song comes on the radio and I wonder if it's one you loved
John Denver sings of lament and I feel his sense of loss
I wonder how many things I never asked
And I know you would not want me to torture myself over your death
I will because that is who I am about such things
There are things in life you never get over
You learn to live with them as you grow old together
There are days when the weight lessens but not enough to forget
It is the gift and the curse of being a human being.

2.2.15...5:54 on the train. John Denver again. Brings out my melancholy

Your Skin

I love feeding you with my touch
There is so much hunger lingering in your eyes
The warmth of your skin against my hands
Brings me more comfort than you can ever know
I want to be everything to you without you having to ask
Ease the burdens of your day and bring your smile back to life
You sigh deeply when my fingers touch your skin
A place deep within you is being awakened
A woman needs to be touched to let her know she has been missed
To let her know how special she is and always will be
A touch can replenish the soul, give you hope to dream
It keeps the darkness of loneliness at bay
The warmth of your body feeds my arousal as we embrace
We are connected because we desire more than just the physical
Our thoughts are making love as our bodies touch fully clothed
There is an intensity that comes from an active imagination
The things I have done to you would make you blush with innocence
When my fingers touch your skin there is transference of energy
You are no longer alone
I am here to comfort you because your happiness is important to me
And because you are mine as you will always be.

2.2.15...3:07 at work
Listening to You Were Meant For Me by Jewel

Give Me

Give me your pain
I will give you my love
Give me your hurt
I will give you kind words
Give me a chance
I will give you my loyalty
Give me your trust
I will give you a friend
Give me your dreams
I help build you a ladder
Give me everything you can
I promise you will never regret
Making the best decision of your life.

2.3.15...8:12 morning
Listening to Come As You Are by Nirvana

This Is Your Life

Sleep is still heavy in your eyes
Your body still tired from yesterday
Life doesn't want to hear your excuses
You need just a few more minutes to get yourself together
The kids need to be fed
You can hear them screaming downstairs
The man of the house is still fast asleep pretending not to hear
This is your life in all its beauty and mess
It is far from glamorous from the outside
Most days you love your family something fierce
They are the jewels in your crown
They keep you sane as the whole world is losing its mind
Right now you are at your breaking point
You are overwhelmed with responsibilities
Robbing Peter to pay Paul when there is no money is an act of Houdini
The kids are oblivious to your stress as it should be when you're that age
Your husband is in constantdenial
Secretly he hopes you can do your superwoman thing
Speak to Jesus and make it all better once again
This time you're not quite sure
Every pot has run dry
Every dollar has been begged and borrowed
Every favor has been returned
You climb out of bed
Drop to your knees and bow your head in prayer
Heavenly father you begin and you feel a hand grasping yours
A family that prays together will find its way through the storm
This is your life
It might not always be glamorous but it is yours to make better.

2.3.15...8:05 its morning time
Listening to Wonder by Nathalie Merchant

When He Is Ready

There is no one to see you crying
Turn up the water to drown out your tears
One step forward then two steps back
There is always an obstacle standing in your way
You bend your knees in prayer
Give thanks for another day of life
There are others who are not as fortunate
You ask of him to give you strength to see beyond your failures
Don't be jealous of your neighbors
Love your family even when they are undeserving
He is preparing you for all your blessings
You are impatient to reap your rewards
But you know God works on his own time
He will let you know when he is ready to give you yours
The work you put in today prepares your success for tomorrow
When he is ready your blessings will come calling
Don't worry about what you cannot control
Just have faith in yourself and the work you have done
Everything else is in God's hands

2.4.15...5:48 on the train
Listening to Take Me To The King by Tamela Mann

Thank You For Caring

Thank you for caring about me
It means so much to know my happiness matters to someone else
You never ask for anything in return
Even though you have your own struggles you put them aside just for me
There must be something you want or need
It is not selfish to want good things for yourself
Giving is its own reward but it's nice to also be appreciated
So tell me friend what I can do for you today
Even if it's a small gesture to show you how much I care
How can I ease the burdens on your shoulders
How can I make your beautiful smile rise on your face
I would love to hear you laugh out loud more often
You don't do that much anymore
I see it in your quiet moments when you become reflective and pensive
Your mood changes and you visit your dark place
The heart cannot hide what it is missing even as you care for others
The world is not your burden to carry
You are not the savior of the universe
You are only one person
Give yourself a break and look around you
Life is happening jump in before it's too late to enjoy the ride.

2.6.15...7:50 in the morning
Listening to Superman by Five For Fighting

Soft Kisser

Your lips look lonely without mines on them
You kiss me with such passion and hunger I forget to breathe sometimes
I don't know where my breath ends and yours begins
I can feel my heart fluttering
My breath quickening with anticipation
The heat in my skin rises to seek your warmth
My heart is open one more time
Your tongue glides across my lips
Something magical is taking place
When you kiss me I cannot explain my physical reaction
It's not like anything I have ever experienced
You take me to places I never imagined I would feel
I become the woman I try to hide but only you can see
You see past my shy facade and the woman in me blossoms like spring
She can finally breathe and is free to express her sensuality
Loving you is contagious
I am addicted to us
It all began with a kiss and slowly the window to my heart opened
You occupy every part of my soul
My fear of not being good enough has been forgotten
You make me feel special
I am no longer invisible, an afterthought
You gave me the courage to find myself
Every day I am discovering something new and wonderful
I just want to thank you for everything you give to me
I just want to thank you for helping me to love myself
I am beautiful.

2.6.15...4:22 on the train
Listening to Thank You by Dido

Greatness

There is greatness alive inside each of us
A talent so beautiful the world would stand up and applaud
Even if your gift is never recognized and given its just due
Even if your name is never known in every part of the world
Even if you live your entire life in relative obscurity
It will not diminish your voice
It will not diminish who you are
A gift is not determined by the acceptance of mass appeal
It is determined by who you have touched
Did the gift of your soul resonate and give someone hope
Did a lost spirit somehow hold on to the next day, the next moment
Something you said, wrote or sang inspired them to fight through the
ennui of life
You might never be great to an uncaring world
But to that one person who needed that hand in the darkness
Those words to soothe a broken heart
To get through to another day
You are a hero even if no one else will ever know
They know because they opened their eyes to see another morning.

2.3.15...6:48 evening.
Listening to Don't Speak by No Doubt

Alternate Universe

We haven't spoken in years now
It doesn't mean I don't speak to you daily
All our conversations are saved
I read your words and it still hurts
Sometimes I trace my fingertips over every syllable
Trying to recall the context of each conversation
The energy of our passion still lives in an alternate universe
Where I imagine you are there waiting for me
And all the misery of these last few years will have been a dream
The dream is shattered when I see you with him
Devastation collides with reality
You are in love
Your smile has returned
Being with me killed its beauty
A small part of me is happy for you
Another part wants him to break your heart
Maybe it's time to retreat to my alternate universe
Where your smile still belongs to me
Where our love is still young and innocent
Our conversations are filled with the passion of lovers
The world becomes less lonely in our alternate universe.

2.6.15...8:12 morning
Listening to Just The Two of Us by Grover Washington Jr.

Ugly Madness

Sometimes I get so angry
I forget to be human and pretend to care about your feelings
My rage is on high and all I want to see is your blood streaming
All I want is to hurt you as deeply as you cut my soul
To cut all the lies from your tongue and see the truth in your eyes
And I find myself screaming at the top of my lungs
I am suffocating on all this filth of pain
Then somewhere inside this ugly madness a quiet descends
This is not who I am
This is what loving you has done to me
A love so toxic should not be able to breathe
It should be strangled and put to sleep
Walking away will not mean you have won
I have chosen to be the bigger person
Even as I fictionalize your death in horrible ways
This ugly madness should not live in a home
It is a spectacle no child should ever have to see
The cycle of this hateful energy will feed on their innocence
I choose to walk away before my anger kidnaps my rational mind
Before I do something that not even time and regret can forgive
For all these reasons
I choose to walk away and declare you the winner.

2.4.15...1:29 in the morning
Listening to The Warrior by Scandal

Fleeting

Happiness so fleeting
My heart is overwhelmed with joy
It feels like I can touch the sky
Catch a ride on a rainbow
Talk to God all in one breath
Maybe he is finally listening
Or is it me who is open to his words
It feels like I have broken through to the other side
This is how the other half lives
I kind of like feeling like this
As if life is something beautiful
Every day is a new adventure
I can wake up every morning my heart is light
My spirit is free
I am happy just to be me
I don't want this feeling to be fleeting
I want it to be my new reality
Once you experience true happiness
It is like the view from the mountaintop
It is like love finally touching your heart
You want to embrace it forever, squeeze it tightly
So when tomorrow comes this new life will still be yours.

2.4.15...3:47 pm
Listening to Joy by Teddy Pendergrass

Safe

I see who you are
I know your heart
It is beautiful like life
You are not hidden to me
You are naked, vulnerable
It is not a weakness to be exposed
With me you are always safe
You can exhale without fear or worry
Your tears will be kissed
I will hold you for as long as you need
Loving me will never hurt
Hurting you would hurt me too much
You are safe
You are where you should be
In my arms and wrapped in love
The safest place in the world.

2.5.15...10:35 at work.
Listening to I'll Be Around by The Spinners

The Other Fairytale

One day you weren't here
Then the next you just appeared
So many nights were spent praying for love
Someone to cherish who I am
Not the fairytale kind of adulation
But the kind of love so real you can feel its quiet energy
You can feel it growing through the years
You know when tough times come it will not disappoint
That kind of sturdy love from a generation long since forgotten
There is a lesson in how they lived their lives
It wasn't always pretty and sexy but you could set your clock by it
A love born of the right stuff does not need constant speeches
It does not need public declarations to feed the ego
It survives through the harshest weather
It finds sunshine even through the darkest winters
Stories are not written about this kind of love
It is not tragically beautiful
The beauty is in its silence
In its ability to be resilient
It keeps finding ways to survive
This kind of love does not inspire beautiful words from poets
But it is the best kind of love you will ever want
It endures when everything else around it has given up
The other fairytale keeps on writing chapters
While the great love story was merely a sonnet.

2.9.15...7:04 New York train
Listening to On The Wings Of Love by Jeffrey Osborne

A Pain That Never Goes Away

Everyone has lost someone close
Years later the pain still breathes in your soul
You are still unable to fully grasp the emptiness
The complete and utter feeling of helplessness
You try to make sense of it all
Death makes no sense even for those with wisdom
It leaves you looking for answers you will never find
Acceptance of the unknowable is the basis of faith
And yet, that just isn't enough to silence the questions
Time they say heals all wounds
Some wounds live a lifetime when you don't have closure
There are moments when the pain is almost too much bear
You pray for death to visit you this evening
All you want is to see your loved one just one more time
One more conversation to let them know they were loved
I guess it's the leaving so much unsaid that's hardest to understand
It's not speaking the truth of your heart when you had the chance
Now all you can do is have a dialogue with yourself
It is a pain that never goes away
Even now as you write this poem there are tears in your eyes
It is a pain that never goes away
But maybe remembering the good times you shared
Can slowly begin to ease that ache in your heart.

2.19.15...6:40 pm on the train
Listening to King of Sorrow by Sade

As Surely

Love spoken into action is just as powerful as words
You love me every day even in silence
There is an energy I feel radiating from your core
It feeds me with such a belief there is no room for doubt
It anchors my soul in this world
Helps me to visualize our future
It gives me wings to unlock my imagination
You have never said you love me
But As surely as I believe in God
I know your love for me is real
I know it does exist.

2.19.15...6:23 on the train.
Listening to I Love You Just Because by Anita Baker

Journey

Our time together is over now
It was a beautiful experience while it lasted
I am ready to move on with my journey
You might not understand why it has to be this way
I cannot explain it to you in a way that would make sense
I just know what I know for myself
I have outgrown this relationship
I crave new challenges and experiences
Pretending otherwise only to spare your feelings would be dishonest
When honesty is what you said you always wanted from me
Truth sometimes comes with a price we pay with our hearts
Maybe one day when you can separate the pain from the truth
When time has calmed your anger
Age has blessed you with wisdom
Maybe then you can find a place in your heart to understand
Staying would have been a prison for me
I would have died an early death
Leaving helped me to spread my wings wider and find myself
It gave you a chance to find real love and not a love based on obligation
And although our journey together is now over
Your impact on my life will never be forgotten
Thank you for gracing my life with your presence
It made me into the person I am today.

2.19.15...10 in the morning
Listening to Stay or Leave by Dave Matthews Band

My Secret

Come a little closer I want to tell you my secret
It's been weighing heavily on my heart for too long now
I seem to have lost my way and there is no map
Maybe I lost it a long time ago and did not even know
I seem to have lost my will to live
And it's not that I want to die and become a martyr or something
More so it is an acceptance of my circumstance,
My allotted place in this world
Once upon a time I had dreams that touched the sky
I believed the silent words written in my heart
I whispered them like a prayer throughout my travels
I am not sure when it happened or even the exact second
But I stopped believing in myself
The world told me I was nothing special
The world showed me that dreams are buried like corpses daily
It's hard to admit to someone that you feel this way
So it's a good thing no one really listens anymore
I have told you my secret
Please take it to your grave
If anyone asks me the truth
I will flash my smile and tell them exactly what they want to hear
They will feel better knowing that they asked
And can go back to their regularly scheduled life
With a clear conscience fully intact.

2.19.15...6:06 on the train
Listening to Grey Street by Dave Matthews Band

Your Smile

Your smile is what I always think of first
Whenever the blues are playing heavy on my heart
I can feel its warmth and energy giving me strength
Urging me to break on through to the other side
Even though we haven't seen each other in years
You are always close in my heart
Never too far away in my mind
It gives me solace when nothing else can
My faith is somehow reaffirmed
Your smile is the closest thing to seeing God
Somehow in those precious seconds when it reveals its beauty
I believe again
As I once did when I was a child.

2.20.15...6:05 train
Listening to One In A Million You by Larry Graham

Pleasure is Coming

My hands love touching your skin
My lips love tasting your kisses
I love taking my time when we make love
There is never a need to rush the inevitable
Pleasure is coming
It could take all morning
Maybe late into a blissful evening
The sounds you make are music to my ears
It is a symphony of colorful words and sounds
The rhythm of your passion is a savage beast
I know your body as if I created it myself
Your passion was lying dormant
Until I lit the flame that rocked your world
Nothing has been the same ever since that day
Your pleasure is coming so glorious and beautiful
It is an honor to bear witness to the creation of love so soulful.

2.23.15...8:04 on the training
Listening to Juicy Fruit by Mtume

First Kiss

There is this thing that happens with us men
When we kiss a beautiful woman for the first time
It feels as if we are awakening from a deep sleep
The world has somehow shifted around us
Everything we believed in no longer exists
Her lips are like the first rays of sunlight soft on your lips
They are like a morning cup of coffee jolting you into reality
Even though we may appear unaffected
Our words never fully expressing our emotions
Something definitely happened
A kiss without any words being spoken
Is the first step into giving love a chance to enter your heart.

2.25.15...8:08 in the morning
Listening to Kiss by Prince

The Dreamer

Another eight hours of a job you hate
Well hate is a strong word but it's how you feel
Every day you have to pretend to be an adult
You do what's necessary to survive
Adults have responsibilities
Society doesn't pay you to dream on the job
Inside you are dying a slow death as the hours tick by
The dreams you had for yourself are fading into the sunset
But there is still a dreamer raging inside of you
The child who refuses to die no matter the odds
So you suck it up and put on your armor to face the world
Only you can kill your dreams
Only you have the final say on your epitaph
As long as there is breath in your body
As long as you believe the impossible can become a reality
The odds are not in your favor
The decks are stacked against you
Times like these are when you reach deeper to find your faith
To find that anchor to carry your dreams to a future
A future you can only see in your mind
But it's as real as the fear you feel every morning
The voice of failure whispers in your ears
Your dreams are gaining strength
They are not as far away as they once were
Stay the course
Call on the strength of your ancestors
Do not give in to the critics of the day
You are not better, but you are just as good as anyone else
Hold on tightly to your dreams
Sometimes they are all you own in this world
They will sustain you through the darkest times
When the good times come because surely they will
Those days of doubt will be just a memory, but always a part of you.

2.24.15...8:17 am...Listening to On & On by Erykah Badu

Inarticulate

Your kisses leave me inarticulate
Unable to form complete sentences
My mind is racing with deep, profound thoughts
But the words from my mouth taste foreign on my lips
Kiss me again exactly the same way you just did
Please don't change anything at all
Right down to your hands on the small of my back
The way your lips softly brush against mine
Goosebumps rise on my skin
I have been waiting for this kiss all my life
I don't where I am right now
Or even how we got here
You kiss me so beautifully I let go of my senses
Trusting in the magic of the moment to keep me safe
My mind is floating away
Clouds are slowly drifting in every direction
I am oblivious because your kisses have woken me up
I will never be the same ever again
And it is all your fault
Kiss me again and I will forgive you.

2.24.15...6:03 on the train
Listening to No One Can Love You More by Phyllis Hyman

Soft Words

Soft words ease deliciously from your mouth
Soothes my thoughts with its gentle touch
Each syllable spills warmly from your lips
Catching a ride on your tongue
I swallow every single word you utter
And it is all I can do to remain calm
The effect you have on me is indescribable
My friends would call me a liar if I tried to explain
Things like this simply do not happen they would say
But it does when we are together
It is all that matters to keep feeling so amazing.

2.26.15...4:39 pm
Listening to A Long Walk by Jill Scott

Spiraling

Hold me close that is what I need right now
Give me your optimism until I can find my faith
I seem to have lost mine somewhere along the way
The world is getting smaller and smaller
I cannot seem to catch my breath,
Spiraling from moment to moment
I need something to anchor my life, a cause
A meaning beyond my own happiness
My own immediate melancholy state of mind
I need to understand life and all the bigger questions
It's making me crazy that nothing makes senseanymore
Life waves by in a blink of an eye
From childhood to being a responsible adult
I just want to take a break from it all
Go back to the days when everything was easy
Maybe not easy, but less of all of *this*
And I know you have things to do today
I am grateful that you took the time to care
Not everyone these days would stop and be a friend
Maybe one day I can return the favor
If life ever gets to be too much and it feels like you're drowning
Pick up the phone, day or night, it doesn't matter
I will be glad to listen to your problems, even if that's all I can do
Hopefully I can get you to that moment where despair does not overwhelm
You can see the light not too far away on thehorizon
Keep walking it's closer than you think sometimes.

2.23.15....12:22 at work
Listening to Hallelujah by Jeff Buckley

Until You Were Gone

I didn't know until you were gone
It never occurred to me you would ever leave
Not because of any perceived arrogance on my part
There are some things unimaginable like death
Losing you felt like the incarnation of such a profound loss
One day we were sharing conversations and ideas
The next day just deafening silence
Even though I could not accept the void of your presence
I remained defiant and waited for your return
I didn't fully realize how deeply you were embedded in my life
Just how much I leaned on you for support
Just how much I would miss the sound of your sensual voice
Just how much I would miss the encouragement of your words
Hearing the laughter in your smile made you feel so much closer
Just how much I would miss hearing you say my name made me feel
so alive
There were things about you I took them for granted,
Not because of any feelings of expectations, but more because we felt
so natural
It never felt like effort because it was so effortless being with you
You anticipated my moods and heard my thoughts through my silence
Your body fit into my embrace as we would kiss with passion
My hands on your skin, on your face, on your lips set me on fire
Even though we were fully clothed you were always naked to me, revealed
The weeks turned into months and you were living your life without me
A part of me was missing and could not be replaced
I stayed in the shadows watching, dissecting the smile on your face
The light in your eyes which once shone for me
Many nights jealousy would ravage my mind
Wondering about things that drove me crazy
Was another touching your soul as deeply as I once did
Was your mind being fed and nurtured by someone more deserving
Was your body being pleasured deep into evening's darkness
My mind was in limbo, the daily torment of your silence
Melancholy turned to anger, then indifference and back and forth
surfed my emotions
And then one day, I opened my eyes and the sun had broken through
the clouds

The radiance of your smile once again blessed me with its presence
The aura of your love humbled me very deeply
You are a blessing I might not deserve but I am grateful you are in my life
Until you were gone,
I never knew how much I needed you
And now you are gone again
This time I fear you won't be returning.

5.5.14…3:42pm…Listening to The Answer Is You by Phyllis Hyman

Catch My Breath

Poetry is my soul food
It feeds my melancholy moods
It guides me through the sea of my discontent
The darkness swallows me and I cannot even breathe
She is my savior when I am drowning
The only one who understands that silence is just as good
When I feel life slipping away like evening into early morning
Like a soul leaving a tired body
When the voices inside my head get so loud they forget I am there
Poetry saves me from the destruction of myself
The voices slowly turn into a conversation
I allow myself a moment to catch my breath
The moment becomes less immediate
The flash of a memory long since forgotten
Eases the stress in my mind
My heart feels lighter again
The people I love are reaching out from beyond
Placing their love all around me
Protecting me from myself
Until the cloud has passed and I can catch my breath.

3.3.15...7:49 on the train
Listening to Something Beautiful by Alexi Murdoch

Held

Your spirit needs to be held
Touched ever so softly with love
I feel you are in need of comfort
Come here allow me to fill that empty space
There is nothing you need to do right now,
Just accept what I want to share
A kiss on your eyelids to make you smile
Another one on your nose makes you laugh out loud
Close your eyes, exhale
I am here for you now
Let go of all the negative energy
Breathe in my love for you
Let your thoughts take you to your happy place
My only concern is for your happiness
Don't worry about the rest
Tomorrow will be here waiting for you again
But tonight is still ahead of us waiting to reveal its secrets
Come here let me hold you
I have been thinking of this moment all day.

3.9.15...5:42 pm
Listening to We Both Deserve Each Other's Love by L.T.D.

Your Words

Your words are oxygen
Fueling my consciousness
Sending air to my lungs
Supplying blood to my veins
You feed me life with your words
You taught me how to embrace my sexuality
You reached beneath the surface of my humanity
What you write matters to someone
It matters to me
I inhale your thoughts deeply
I keep them stored in my heart
Each word is a sip of wine
The taste inebriates my senses
I imagine the struggle you endure
Fitting the pieces together like a puzzle
It is like unlocking the secrets of the heart
They help me understand who I am
Your words touch me in a way nothing else can.

3.10.15...10:25 at work.
Listening to Here Comes The Sun by The Beatles

Invisible

It's nice to hear you say you love me
You don't say it often anymore
Maybe because you think after all these years I should already know
Sometimes a girl just needs to hear her guy say the words
A little reminder never hurts
You shouldn't say it because of any expectations
You shouldn't say it to keep me quiet
If you need a reason to declare your affections
Then you can keep the words to yourself
And it seems sometimes your words are not discernable
As if you are afraid to express your feelings
You never say you love me first anymore
It is always in response to my declaration
Maybe I am just being a female
I admit I can be emotional at times
But love without emotion seems like such a waste
You will never have to guess my heart belongs to you
After all these years of sharing a life
I don't think it's asking too much of the man I love
Once in a while to make me blush
Say something to make me feel beautiful
Let me know you appreciate my efforts
There is nothing worse than feeling invisible or taken for granted
You were that man once when we fell in love
Share that man with me again.

3.10.15...6:43 rainy evening on the train.
Listening to Wishing On A Star by Rose Royce

You Promised

You promised you would always be there for me
No matter what happened I could depend on our friendship
But sometimes life happens
The best of intentions are quickly forgotten
There is not always blame to place
People grow apart sometimes for no reason
It would easy to blame life for getting in the way
Life is not the culprit this time
We make time for the things we really care about
There are just not enough hours in the day sometimes
Not every promise is meant to be kept
It's good when someone keeps their word because it's who they are
I will not hold you to promises made when the future was still uncertain
Now that we are struggling to hold on to what we believe
In this chaos your word should mean something
I keep hoping for a surprise that the person you were
Will one day resurface for air
And the words you spoke so long ago will once again have meaning.

3.10.15...3:43 pm. Front lobby at work. Raining. Digging Wonderwall by Oasis

Never-ending

Your beauty does not begin with the physical
In fact you are so much more than that to me
When thoughts of you touch my heart
I remember how you treat me as a man
You are the gatekeeper to my dreams
You understand how the world can steal your confidence
You have a subtle way of letting me know
Your belief in me is Never-ending
My dreams are wondrous to behold
But there is nothing more beautiful
Than when a woman believes in her man.

3.10.15...6:29 train delay. Reading The Immortal Life of Henrietta Lacks

Profound

A loss so profound
Years later it still staggers me to my core
It reveals itself in moments which leaves me vulnerable
The cathartic waves of tears stream down my face
It is as if you just died yesterday
The familiar ache is still fresh
Clutching at my heart with its heartfelt memories
This constant emptiness has never been replaced
We carry those we love in our thoughts
The constant conversation which never ends
They remain forever alive
Safe in a world we created
Death cannot extend its reach to steal what is immortal
You remain my friend forever on this journey called life.

3.11.15...7:08 pm.
Listening to Chasing Cars by Snow Patrol

My Body Aches

My body aches to be touched again
Not just by random hands but by onlyyours
You have spoiled me for any other man
You have the hands that heal
The hands that know where my secrets wait in silence
Only the magic of your hands
The supple softness of your lips
Has the power to unleash the savage beast of my femininity
Only you know how to take me to the edge of insanity
And with just one look, a gentle touch
I become myself once again
You have stayed away too long
My body needs tending like a garden needs water
My heart needs affection like a baby needs love
My mind needs to be fed beautiful words of prose
Come back to where you belong
No questions will be asked
No demands will be made
Make love to me softly
Make love to me with an angry fire
A raging inferno of passion
Just make me feel alive and beautiful
Make me feel like I am the only woman in the world that matters.

3.12.15...6:16pm on the train.
Listening to Til The Cops Come Knocking by Maxwell

Fading Into Obscurity

Years have now gone by
Time they say heals all wounds
Like love, time seems to have forgotten about me
I hurt as much as I ever did
Without you I lost everything
Fading into obscurity sometimes it feels as if we never happened
A song whispers on the radio
I reread books we read together
A certain passage pulls on the strings of my memory
That familiar ache returns and tears spill from my heart
I am never getting over you and that is my truth
Even though you have long forgotten about me
Your Facebook status says you are happy and in love
I stalk you quietly from the shadows
No harm is intended to you by me
I just enjoy imagining what could have been
Even though watching your eyes light up for another is torture
What we had has long since faded into obscurity
You are a different person now and all that's left to wonder
What could have been will never be known

3.16.15...6:13 pm
Listening to People Are Strange by The Doors

Insecure

The days when I doubted myself are in my past
Gone is the insecure young woman you took for granted
You treated me like your property
I turned to you to boost my low self-esteem
It only fed your fragile male ego
You felt like such a man telling all your friends you had me trained
You never viewed me as a person
I was just a possession for your amusement
You kept me dependent on your love and sex
Rationed it until it became a drug
It was something I needed to have, even though it did me harm
I needed to have your approval or else I felt worthless
You knew just how to manipulate my obedience
My thoughts in my head was your voice
My needs were always about your pleasure
I didn't know who I was
I was only somebody because you told me so
When I was of no use to you anymore
You tossed me aside without a second thought
You did me a favor without even knowing
You forced me to look at who I had become
Many nights I felt like the woman you had created
The eyes in the mirror belonged to someone else
When you have nowhere left to turn
No more excuses to defend your actions
You stand up and hold yourself accountable for all your mistakes
In my honesty I found my strength
The caterpillar turned into a butterfly
My legs turned into wings
My tears and anger turned into prayer
The woman I was slowly died
From the ashes I was reborn
Strong, black and beautiful
I determined my own purpose
I answer to only one man, my savior
The journey was hard but I made it through

I am standing on the other side of pain
The view through the eyes of happiness is beautiful.

6:49 pm...3.24.15
Listening to Golden by Jill Scott

Something About You

There is just something about you
I enjoy without defining it by name
It is an absolute joy to indulge you in conversation
Your eyes light up when we discuss subjects of passion
Your laughter is always infectious
I can feel it making its way through my defenses
You arouse my mind with the thoughts you have
Your beauty is boundless
It is not defined by our culture
It is something natural born of the earth
I hope you know how beautiful you are
I have told you countless times before
It is that rare beauty that encompasses not only the physical
It makes you believe that everything is possible
People like you are a rare find in an unoriginal world
Please never change
The world needs beauty like yours.

8:22 am...3.25.15
Listening to Satisfy My Soul by Bob Marley

There Are Moments

There are moments in the day when I think of us
All these questions of life and love
Where would we be if fate hadn't intervened
Would you be happier without me
Me without you
Is all of this just random occurrences
We as humans do the best with what we are given
And then I wonder when I gravitate to your thoughts
Do you still smile sometimes because I make you happy
Or do you ever wonder if you made the right decision staying
It's not an easy question to ask of each other
It is the elephant in the room sucking all the oxygen
The truth is now dressed in gray
Answers are hedged
Half-truths are told
Feelings would be hurt if the truth of the heart is revealed
A life filled with ambiguities corrodes the soul
It steals the possibility of living an authentic life
Whatever the truth might be waiting in the shadows to be told
Speak yours without malice of thought
Only then can you reclaim everything you have lost.

8:04 on the train...3.25.15
Listening to She's Always A Woman by Billy Joel

More Than Good Enough

Behind that beautiful she hides so much sadness
I want to let her know it's okay to feelmelancholy
Let the tears flow
Give your smile a rest
No one expects you to be everyone's strength
Give yourself a break, exhale
Sadness is only temporary
Your future is waiting to embrace your passion
Don't focus on the moment
Look out and see the big picture
I promise you have not been forgotten
You have too much to offer the world
If not the world, then one person at a time
You can make a difference
I know this,
I have seen glimpses of your greatness
You just have to believe you are more than good enough.

3.25.15...1:36 pm
Listening to Here Comes The Sun by George Harrison

Every Woman

Don't assume you know who I am
I am many women wrapped up in one
I am the mother who would die for her children
I am the wife who loves her husband and always has his back
I am the friend who will always tell you the truth even when it's hard
I am complicated with my thoughts
I am joyful when I laugh
I love hard, I cry easily
My will is strong,
My reserve is deep
My memory is long but my heart is forgiving
Don't assume you know who I am after oneconversation
There are many layers beyond the physical
I have lived, loved, been hurt and even broken a few hearts along the way
I am not fragile but I am still a woman
Don't underestimate my femininity for weakness
As I don't assume your maleness as strength
My desires are not some deep dark secret
All you have to do is ask and I shall share
I want a life where I am free to be myself
A man who is strong enough and not threatened to stand beside me
When the time comes to stand behind me as I will do for him
I want a home filled with love
When anger invades its tranquility we are grown enough to work it out
The world is busy these days and filled with too much noise
What once was special is now taken for granted
Everything has a price and can be bought
There are some things that should be sacred, priceless
Hold me in the highest regard as I do you always
Treat me the way I deserve because I have earned it
I am every woman but I will always be yours
As long as you honor me, As long as you love me
As long as you respect me
Everything I have, Everything I am
Begins and ends with our love.

5:13 pm...3.25.15
Listening to I'm Every Woman by Whitney Houston
(Love the Chaka Khan version also)

Illusions

You don't care about me anymore
Maybe you never did but you were a fantastic actor
You don't even call to see how I am
Somehow I thought we would remain friends
But I guess that's just the woman in me thinking the best of you
Maybe it's all for the best I see you as you are
No illusions of what's been lost
You got what you wanted without caring about what I needed
I cannot even say you used me
I knew who you were and I opened my heart to let you in
I thought in time you would change
That the love of a good woman is all you needed
I thought no one could understand you like me
You treated me like all the others
I blame no one but myself
I saw something in you that just wasn't there
The illusions are gone
The facade has finally lifted
In time I will be thankful that you left me
But for right now
I miss you every single second of every single day.

8:21 am...3.27.15
Listening to What You Won't Do For Love by Bobby Caldwell

Dream Not Deferred

Come on over here
It is not as bad as it seems
Don't let being disillusioned kill your dreams
Life has a way of balancing things
Rewards your determination when least expect
And I know all your hard work seems unappreciated
You cannot seem to catch a break no matter how hard you try
It seems like the world is against you
Everyone has left you behind
You are better off just squandering your talents
When that thought poisons your mind
Remember the times you felt joy doing what you love
How it felt when someone was inspired by what you created
And I know it's hard when you want to give up
The quest for greatness can be a lonely journey
If you do it because you love it
Because it feeds your soul
The riches will come in many unexpected ways
Follow the path in your heart
The way is already illuminated for you.

7:08 pm...3.25.15
Listening to Wake Up Everybody by Teddy Pendergrass

Tell Me

Tell me how much you miss me
I want to feel the words when you say them
I need to know when we are apart
That sometimes you feel lost and it's hard to admit
When you see me again there is an unspoken joy youfeel
When you wrap your arms around me I need to know I am home
I need to know I am safe
The world moves fast these days
There seems to be no time to enjoy leisurely things
Quiet moments spent enjoying each other's company
A glass of wine mixed with good conversation
The world is quiet and it's just us even for a few hours
Moments like that help to rejuvenate my spirit
I need those things from you
If I go too much longer without feeling connected
I fear I will begin to slowly drift away.

7:17 pm...3.26.15
Listening to Lead Me Into Love by Anita Baker

The Weekend

It has been a long hard week seemingly without end
Your mind is fatigued and your body is tired
All you want right now is some peace and quiet
A bubble bath and a glass of wine to complete the picture
It would be nice to hear no one calling your name for once
The phone remains silent and no friends needing advice
You just want to be forgotten for the weekend
Invisible as you spend some time with yourself
We live in a society which values constant motion even if it's just a
facade
Slowing down the pace is viewed as falling behind
Everyone is trying to keep up but with what is the big mystery
You leave the world behind when the door closes
You exhale as you get undressed, reveling in your nakedness
The only sound you will hear for the next two days is silence
No cell phones or television
No computers or human beings
Just the solace of your own beautiful company
You can get lost in that book you've been wanting to read forever
Watch that old movie again from your childhood
There is no time like the present to indulge yourself when needed.

3.27.15....6:58 pm
Listening to Slow Down The Pace by Gregory Isaac

Dysfunctional Marriage

Something akin to hate now lives in this house once filled with love
There is no escaping this suffocating feeling anymore
You used to wonder how couples got to this point in a marriage
Why not simply walk away and leave it all behind
Material things are accumulated
Ugly thoughts once silent are now spoken
Your facade of a happy couple long since forgotten
Lines are drawn and there is going back to what used to be
You don't recognize this person you have become
You have to win at all cost, even though you have already lost
Your home should be your place of sanctuary
Every day you open your front door and put on your armor
You put away your smile and prepare for battle
The wounds from these verbal and sometimes physical altercations are
hidden in your smile
Your laughter once filled with life, now seems empty and forced
You are too young to be this tired
You are too strong to be this beaten
You have given your all in this marriage
Being a martyr is not your destiny
Walk away before it's too late
Before the darkness of anger clouds your judgment
What once was good in this marriage has long since died
But goodness still lives in your heart
It is waiting to flourish once again
You just have to find the strength to leave this dysfunctional marriage.

4.6.15...9:06 am
Listening to On My Own by Patti LaBelle & Michael McDonald

Edge of Insanity

Kisses on my skin leaves me weak
Your lips search slowly for my secret places
Each time one is discovered I cry out in sheer ecstasy
This feeling of being on fire consumes me to no end
I don't want you to stop even when my screams have gone silent
This body is yours to do as you please
Please be gentle in my moments of uncertainty
When you feel the tide of desires rising and I am near drowning
Take me to the edge of insanity,
Show me the world in all its beauty through your eyes
Give me a glimpse into what makes you so beautiful
Take me in your arms and whisper your heart to me
Until my dreams are magical once again.

11.30 am... 4.4.15
Listening to Day Is Done by Nick Drake

Awakened

Senses once dormant are now awakened
My mind was sleeping before you kissed me
My body never imagined pleasure like this was possible
No man has ever kissed me like that before
Shivers ran through my body
My soul sighed deeply
My desires outraced my thoughts and circled back again
Arousal made me too weak to think straight
Ever since that day I am not the same woman
I thought I had experienced passion before you came along
I know now there is a difference
It was like having an out of body experience
I felt myself floating away and not even caring
I just wanted this feeling to last forever
You awakened a side of me I didn't know existed
And now I am always hungry for more of your love.

4.15.15...2:58 on the train
Listening to She's Always a Woman by Billy Joel

Breakfast Smells Good

Breakfast smells good this morning
You are cooking my favorite things
Lazy Saturday mornings are made for sleeping in late
Catching up on the week and missed conversations
Maybe later we will go back to bed and cuddle naked
Your back is turned to me when I enter the kitchen
You are singing a song out of tune but it sounds beautiful to me
You feel my presence and greet me with a smile
A smile all these years later still makes my heart flutter
The heat from your body presses into mine as I kiss your neck
It is a familiar scent of comfort that humbles me with gratitude
You never gave up on me even when you could
Words of affection and love spill from my heart
The heat from your lips warms my ear
Breakfast is almost ready
I make your coffee just the way you like
We sit down with books in hand,
Ready to be transported to another place and time
Always knowing this world is where we will always have each other.

4.18.15...nine in the morning
Listening to Say You Won't Let Go by James Arthur

Life's Compromise

I feel my life drifting by
My thoughts are all over the place
I am unable to connect with the things which were once important
And it's not because I don't care anymore
Disappointments can mute your efforts to get ahead
There is so much you want to do
When you were younger there weren't any obstacles
You were always up for the challenge
The older version of you now realizes
There are some things you must let go
Letting go helps you to move forward
Some call it giving up
You simply call it compromise and doing what you must
There are still some days when you feel that spark of excitement
Wanting to give it just one more try
You look at your life and the cloud descends
You are responsible for others now
The luxury of being carefree is no longer your choice
It's now a life of compromises
You still have your dreams
They are always the best company
On days when you feel invisible and unimportant
They still make you feel special because they belong only to you.

11:20 in the morning. Mother's Day 5.09.15…1:15 in the afternoon
Listening to White Flag by Dido

She Needs

Every woman needs to be made love to
They need to be touched and made to feelspecial
They need to be touched by an unselfish lover
A man who senses her hunger and feeds it without being asked
He knows where to touch and kiss because he listens to her body
Beneath her words he hears the quiet desires of her heart
Things she would like to say but the fear of rejection keeps her quiet
The price of heart break is too high to pay
Especially if you have felt its wrath once or twice
So she will speak her thoughts to him as they make love
Praying that between her sounds of passion he will listen
Her heart is insistent on something deeper
She has grown tired of superficial expressions of love
Her cries need a place to call home
Her heart deserves a place where it is safe
She hopes that this man is unlike the others
He can hear not only the passion of her body
But feel all the love that is waiting for him.

12:01 afternoon. 5.09.15
Listening to Just Let Go by James Bay

The Silence of Your Thoughts

There is nothing we need to say right now
Let us just be quiet and enjoy the moment
The silence is music if you listen close enough
The hum of your thoughts
The steady beat of your heart
Your dreams in the background provides inspiration
Life is too loud these days
Everyone's so busy always in a rush
There seems to be no time for contemplation, introspection
So many distractions to interrupt the beauty
Silence is a beautiful thing when you embrace the simple concept
It allows you to still your spirit
Take a breath for a moment
Slow down the world around you
Have a conversation with yourself
Things you missed become clearer now
You begin to understand your motivation as you listen to your thoughts
The things we crave the most in this life comes at no cost
You just have to decide between the life you want and who you really are
Sometimes they travel on different paths
In the silence of your thoughts examine who you want to be
Find the peace that the world cannot give you
It has to come from a place only you know and love.

5.13.15...8:54 in the morning
Listening to She's Gone by Hall & Oates

Happy Emptiness

Everyone thinks I am happy
Maybe that's my fault for portraying that image
They mistake my sunshine smile for happiness
Lost are the dark clouds behind my eyes
My laughter makes them jealous of my life
They see all the material possessions but not the hard work
Hidden behind it is a deep profound emptiness
It's all smoking mirrors and lies
A carefully crafted facade to hide the truth
I am lonely and crave affection
Not that superficial stuff performed for company
But the kind that makes my soul leap in anticipation
The kind that makes me want to give more of myself and not feel used
I glide through my days being everything to everyone
I am the friend you call when you need advice
Your ride or die when you have to handle your business
Maybe it's the adrenaline rush of feeling needed
It helps me to forget all the things I don't have
If someone asked me the right question when I feel vulnerable I
might shed the facade for once and allow them to see mypain.

5.13.15...10:23 in the morning
Listening to Love Won't Let Me Wait by Luther Vandross

Sweet Words

Her eyes light up when she hears his voice
A sudden shift in her aura from dark to light
Anyone watching can tell she is a woman in love
Sweet words are softly kissing her ears
Opening her heart to fill it with joy
She is beautiful to watch in moments like these
She laughs easily now without a care in the world
She is transforming right before their very eyes
A beautiful butterfly spreading its wings
Taking flight into the clear blue sky
Beauty so effortless can make your heart stop and skip a beat.

5.14.15....5:28 pm
Listening to Falling In and Out of Love by Pure Prairie League

Nostalgia

I want to go home but home does not exist anymore
All my friends have moved away
Some have passed on before their time
But when is it ever your time to die
It always your time to live
The place is different now
The essence of community and respect are gone
Home is now just a place I knew as a child
Nostalgia now makes me smile when I recall
Random memories now bring me joy
It is a place kept safe in my heart
We can only ever revisit our childhood through old friends
They remind you of good times and conversation
Pranks played and things you have long since forgotten
A time when your worries were few and inconsequential
The world felt like a better place
Maybe it wasn't but you didn't know any better
Your parents protected you from the world
There is no added security in knowledge
And now evil seems too close for comfort these days
Nostalgia gives you a reprieve
Just a moment when you can forget and indulge
But you can only live in the past for so long
Eventually you have to rejoin the world and become an adult.

5.20.15...3:37 afternoon. Let Her Go by Passenger

Sweet Innocence

You kiss me as if you are starving for love
As if you don't know how beautiful you are
As if your lips have not been kissed in years
A deep hunger in your soul needs to be fed
I can taste the tears on your lips
I can see the hope in your eyes
I can feel all the love in your heart
Take your time I am here for as long as you need
I will feed you for as long as you want
You breathe in my scent like oxygen
Storing it deep inside your memory
I am feeding your desire to be held and seen
You are not invisible to me
I see the beauty of who you are
Your feelings matter because I care for you
Your body trembles in anticipation of what comes next
The gentle quiver of your lips reminds me of sweet innocence
I want to protect you from everything that will break your heart
Each kiss peels back layers of years of being untouched
Of years of falling asleep all alone and unloved
The way you delicately kiss me savoring every drop
Almost brings me to the verge of tears
Your skin against mine will be forever etched in my memory
How warm you felt
The moment is over because all moments eventually end
But you are now part of my history
Every moment will be measured against you.

5.26.15...4:46 pm Listening to Home by Stephanie Mills

Mid-Life Crisis

Sometimes I find it hard to breathe
The world is spinning out of control all around me
I have to remind myself to exhale so I don't get overwhelmed
It feels like I am in this all alone
It feels like I have nowhere to turn for advice
I don't know how to make this right
Is it even worth trying anymore
The only thing that keeps me going sometimes is knowing
There has to be more than just this emptiness
This constant feeling of never being good enough
I didn't always feel this way about myself
Once upon a time I was happy or hope that I was
So I imagine there is still time for change
I imagine others are going through this mid-life crisis
I can't be the only one filled with doubt,
Of the road not chosen
No one expresses sentiments like these to each other anymore
It's always happy smiles and drinks
They are always filled with such confidence
Everyone is on that train to happy
They must have inside knowledge
Someone please share with me
I am drowning and there is no water around
I am crying but no one dries my tears
I am lost in broad daylight
Maintaining the facade has left me exhausted
I just want to figure this thing out
So I can feel like everyone else.

5.27.15...10:38 in the morning
You Make Loving Fun by Fleetwood Mac

Fatigue

My life hurts to live
And it's not that I am not thankful for all I have
Maybe I am a little bit selfish for wantingmore
I want the dreams in my head to be real
I want the love I deserve to be worthy of my heart
I am fatigued from trying and always being this good person
I am always the one who is thinking of everyone's feelings
What about me for once?
When do I get pampered and fussed over?
When do I finally matter?
When does someone love me as much as I love them?
I know all the answers to these questions
When you're alone the answers don't keep youwarm
They don't make you feel special
I am fatigued
I just want to sleep for a bit
Maybe I will wake up and all of this will have just been a dream.

5.27.15....ten in the morning
Listening to Can't You See by The Marshall Tucker Band

When

When there is nothing left in the world except silence
When there are no more thoughts to have
When there is no more love to give
When there is no one left to hate
When there is no more sadness left to feel
When there is nowhere left to run
When there is no more lies to be told
When the truth no longer matters
When it is too late to forgive
When there are no tears left to cry
When there is no more laughter to be heard
When all your dreams have been reached
When all your dreams have slipped through your fingers
When there are no more chances to be given
When you are too tired to even care
Will we finally understand how beautiful this life could have been
If you had just enjoyed the ride before it was over

5.27.15...3:46 pm
Listening to If You Read My Mind by Gordon Lightfoot

Ugly Heart

If you cannot give me what I need then why are you in my life
I am too grown for childish mind games
I need more than sex to make me happy
More than empty promises to fill my heart
You can take that shit somewhere else and leave me alone
I have gotten over better men than you before
Being in love does not make me blind to who you are
Good loving doesn't excuse your bad behavior
Your smile might be beautiful
Your swagger presidential
Your loving does magical things to my body
But your heart is ugly
If I allow myself to be mesmerized by your seductive charm
I can't blame anyone but myself for being so weak
You know how to push my buttons
Make me speak in tongues of passion
Every time I say it's the last time
You do that thing again and resisting you is futile.

5.30.15...5:49 on the track
Listening to More Than A Feeling by Boston

A New You

Everyone is meant to be loved
Everyone has a purpose to fulfill in this life
Even when you believe love has forsaken you
Love cannot find you when you are cloaked in darkness
It cannot find you when you allow yourself to remain lost
There are reasons for your unhappiness in your situation
Simply finding love cannot make it all better
You have to examine the root of your problems
Shine a light on it without any excuses
Own up to your mistakes without blaming others
Plant a new seed
Create a new you
A better version of learned experiences
Light gravitates to light
Love wants to be in love
It only blooms when your spirit is open
Who you want to be is right below the surface
Waiting for you to recognize what you already have
Don't keep your life waiting too much longer
You only have so much time left on this Earth to get it right.

5.30.15...5:36 on the track
Listening to Faithfully by Journey

Passing Time

There is a part of me that has remained untouched
Impatiently waiting for a man who is deserving
I have never given all of myself to anyone
Maybe it's because I knew they were undeserving of my love
Maybe I knew they would only be passing time
A man who is only interested in your body and not your mind
Will always find another warm bed to occupy
My love is not an easy thing to handle
I am a woman who wants to give as much as she gets
I am tired of settling for less than I deserve
I know my worth and if you can't afford it
Please find another heart to play with
My heart wasn't made for passing time
It is ready to be treasured forever.

5.30.15....5:24 on the track
Listening to On and On by Stephen Bishop

Crying Orgasm

You trace your lips over my bare skin
My body surrenders to your touch
Shuddering in submission of pleasure to come
My blood boils, waiting to escape
I keep my eyes closed,
As if that will make it more intense, and it does.

6.3.15...2:15 on the elevator
Listening to Sexy M.F. by Prince

Defenseless

Something comes over me and I am left defenseless
My emotions leave me naked in your presence
I want to hide but I need you to see who I am
I want you to see the woman I am when we make love
How you touch my spirit so deeply tears run freely
I am left open like a wound that I don't want to ever heal
The rawness of my emotions is empowering to my soul
I am a woman on fire for her lover
See what you have done to me
You awakened a part of me I did not even know existed
Now that I have found myself
I can never go back to who I once was.

6.3.15...5:45 pm walking to the train
Listening to Fortunate by Maxwell

Solitude

My time alone is valuable
It is how I calm my spirit
Sort through my discontent
Allowing me to disconnect from the world
So I can find my happy place once again
There are days when it cannot be found
A turbulent world can infiltrate even the most serene place
Then there are days like today when simple things make me happy
I am thankful to see the sun shining
Happy to hear the laughter of my children
Feel the love of my husband
I am thankful to God and all his blessings
I hold on to these things because even when you are blessed
You can still feel lost in this world
You can still feel without purpose
Doubts will sometimes cloud your mind
Old insecurities are never too far away
I ride the emotional wave of life and wait for the calm
The secret to life is keeping it all in perspective
Nothing is as urgent as it seems
The answers are always there waiting to be found
Solitude allows me time with my thoughts
A much needed break from the chaos of the world.

6.8.15...1:24 pm
Listening to Poems, Prayers & Promises by John Denver

Take Care of Yourself

Take care of yourself
Even though we didn't work out
I always want the best for you in life
Maybe I couldn't make you happy even though I tried
There always seemed to be something missing
You were always searching and needing something that wasn't me
It's not anything you ever said
You were never disrespectful
You never expressed your anger by being physical
You were affectionate but never too much
You were present but always with some distance to run
I wanted so much for you to love me
You never gave us a chance
You were always haunted by someone I couldn't compete with
A love from your past who has moved on but left you stuck
A woman can only wait around for so long before she has had enough
You are a good man
I am a good woman
We are just not good together and maybe never were
Take care of yourself
Once in a while call to see how I'm doing
I will do the same for you
Take care of yourself.

6.5.15...8:16 am
Listening to Dreams by Fleetwood Mac

Tired

Sometimes I just get so tired
Every bit of energy leaves my body
And I know there are people worse off than me
My burdens are not too heavy to carry
I would just like to know how it feels when everything clicks
When the struggles are a thing of the past
When all your hard work has finally paid off
Until that day arrives I must continue to persevere
Find strength from those who came before
A legacy isn't built on giving up
A family doesn't prosper if you don't find a way
You might not feel it yet but your second wind is coming
A gentle breeze is blowing to shorten the distance
Being tired is never an excuse for giving up on your dreams
You are almost at the finish line so see it through
Whatever happens you can hold your head up high.

6.8.15...10:33 pm
Listening to It's Too Late by Carole King

Ain't It Funny

Ain't it funny when a woman is lonely
Her phone forgets to ring,
No one is calling to sweep her off her feet
You're her best friend in the world
She calls you every day just to say hello she says
Until someone shows her attention
And then you are once again forgotten
Being in love or something close to that
Makes some women lose their minds
And it's not that your feelings are hurt
Maybe they are just a bit
You are happy for your friend because everyone deserves to be happy
But you've been down this road before
Love often times goes wrong and when it does
Your old friend will come calling once again
With not so much as an apology for taking you for granted
Ain't it funny how friendships sometimes work
A one way street with no intersections for you to get off.

6-14-15…1:38 pm
Digging some Silly Love Songs by Wings

Come Here

Before you go and leave me craving your taste
Say what your heart wants to reveal
I taste your words in every kiss
I relish how you murmur when our tongues touch
Your heart is on display when you purr so softly
Your lips cannot keep a secret from me
Your body betrays your every thought
I know you are in love with me
Both of us have been hurt before
It is a road we have walked before
The signs are everywhere that failure is imminent
But love does not adhere to past failings
Only the now is important
The past is no longer relevant
If you can get it right just once
Nothing else will ever matter

6.14.15...4:41 in the afternoon
Listening to Goodbye Stranger by Supertramp

Amazing Lover

Soft kisses make you tremble uncontrollably
Feels like an earthquake shattering your senses
You are an amazing lover to behold
You are giving without being asked
It makes me want to please you even more
To find a place we have never visited and make it ours
Just merely being in your presence makes me catch my breath
It is all I can do sometimes not to surrender to my desires
In the presence of company we make love in my mind
Waiting for the moment until we are alone again
All my thoughts then become a reality
Making love to you is an experience without words
It has to be felt to be fully understood.

6.14.15...4:27 pm
Listening to Laughter In The Rain by Neil Sedaka

Contagious

Your fire is contagious
Its sets me aflame with just one look
I can feel your desire simmering in your skin
You give me that look and I know I am in trouble
You are ready to erupt
It's been too long since you've been touched like this
Too long since you've allowed your mind to travel
Too long since your body has felt this good
Relax you are in good hands this evening
Relinquish all control to your desires
I know what you need so please don't worry
One evening begins the journey to forever.

6.14.15...4:13 pm
Listening to Rhiannon by Fleetwood Mac

Take Me To Church

Within these walls you are safe
Leave all your troubles behind
Raise your voice in prayer
Embrace the love of God the father
He loves you as you are
You were created in his own image
No pretenses or makeup is needed when you enter his home
Take me to church the congregation sings
The air is vibrant with love
Heaven lives in their fervent prayers
Protect us from the evil that lurks in the hearts of men
Show us the way some of us have forgotten
When evil comes knocking without any warning
Know that God is watching in your final hour
He weeps for you as if you were his only child
As the light fades and you are called home to be at his side
Your time on Earth is over
Leave all those worries behind
Rejoice in the life you've lived
Now comes the hereafter
Take me to church the choir sings
Take me to the house of my Father
All is well in his house of love.
Take me to church...

6.18.15...9:33 in the morning
I wrote this piece this morning on the train as I thought about
those 9 innocent lives murdered in church, their sanctuary.
Listening to Just A Closer Walk With Thee by Mahalia Jackson

Bow

We bow our heads in prayer
Ask God to look after our sons and daughters
To watch over them as they travel through this world
Unspeakable evil walks this earth
Cloaking its deeds under the guise of being righteous
But faith, hope and love is our armor
There is still goodness to be found all around us
Even though there are no guarantees of returning home safely
We kiss our children goodbye before we leave
An extra hug for our spouses is filled with meaning
With a heart filled with love and hope
We step into the world to live our lives and pray for God's mercy
Until we meet again this evening as a family.

6.21.15...10:45 am
Listening to Precious Lord Take My Hand by Mahalia Jackson

Children

We give our children wings to fly
Food to eat for strength
The determination to take on the world
Courage to do what is right as we lead by example
We watch them grow knowing soon they will be gone
We won't be needed quite as much
It can be a thankless job at times
But we relish the rewards when they come
We worry about them in silence
Just as much as when they were children
Being grown doesn't stop the fear they are still our babies
We worry if we did enough to prepare them for life
We worry if we made it too easy
Did we make it hard too because it's how we were raised
Then there are unexpected moments when it all comes together
You watch this person, your child, doing incredible things
Your heart fills with my pride
Your eyes brim with tears
The road was rough but you persevered
This child of yours, a life so precious and irreplaceable
Thanks you for all your sacrifices made
They vow to always make you proud
You smile to yourself, they already have.

6.22.15...10:22 am
Listening to Heal The World by Michael Jackson

For the Briefest Moment

I breathe you into my senses and place you safely in my heart
Not so I can forget which would be impossible
But so I can remember this moment forever
I want to always remember how you held me so tightly
As if the world was about to end
You wanted me to save you from something I did not yet understand
It was beautiful to feel so wanted
It felt like I was making a difference in your life
I knew eventually the storm would pass and I would not be needed
Whatever drew you to me would soon get better
You would sail on to your eventual destination
I was just a stop along the way
Even though I wished for a different ending for us
I wanted you to be my Prince Charming
I am grateful that our paths crossed for the briefest moment
You awakened the woman inside me I didn't even know was there.

6.22.15...5:49 pm on the train
Listening to Year Of The Cat by Al Stewart

Almost Spiritual

Your body was sculpted by God for my pleasure
Maybe not for me but I am lucky to indulge in all its wonderful secrets
You say words I have never heard whispered before
You make sounds that inspire my creative passion
When I kiss you in certain places
You become this thing, filled with energy, almost spiritual
The universe glows in your skin
The history of life lives in your eyes
It feels good to be part of something so beautiful
Every curve of your body is imprinted in my fingertips
Every moan tasted by my lips
I know you in a way no one ever will
We are connected by a bond that cannot be broken
I have seen you at your most vulnerable, sensual
I have seen you at your strongest and it is admirable
What we shared in those moments is beyond my imagination
It is the stuff of dreams written in erotica novels
The stuff of prose that only a poet can truly capture
It's a spiritual connection with a foundation based on love
It only grows deeper with each root planted
It only gets stronger as the years go on
There is always something amazing to discover aboutyou
It's a journey into the future I am happy to take
Wherever it leads we will take it together
Our love is so much more than just the pleasure of the physical
It is blessed with all the secrets of the spiritual.

6.27.15...9:13 am
Listening to Baker Street by Gerry Rafferty

Held

It feels good to be held again
The simple things you miss when you are single
I suppose married couples can feel that way too
The closeness of human contact be so reassuring
A bond between two people, a silent understanding
It is emotional trust without the explanation of words
Knowing someone will be there for you when the dust settles
You won't have to go at it all alone
It's knowing when you are at your weakest
There is someone to keep you upright, they will not let you fall
When someone holds you and you feel their energy flowing
It renews your strength
The world doesn't seem such a scary place
It fills you with confidence to keep on trying
These are the things which are unspoken but mean so much.

6.26.15...9:19 am
Listening to How Much I Feel by Ambrosia

Happiness

Happiness stared at me one morning and smiled
You have been searching for me for so long now
Every time you find me you try so hard to do everything right
In doing so you forget yourself
You forget the lessons of the past
You cannot fit happiness into a box and bend it to your will
Happiness is free and cannot be manipulated to create moments
You have to relax and stop constantly worrying where I am
Embrace the life you have been given without always wondering
Stop comparing yourself to others and wanting what they have
Happiness is the absence of want
It is knowing that what you have is all you need in this moment
Happiness is being able to make due with less than needed
Once you understand the secret to finding happiness
You won't have to go searching the four corners of the world
It was always right there with you waiting to be found.

6.28.15...1:21pm
Listening to Sara Smile by Hall & Oates

Struggle

Sometimes you feel so alone in this world
It feels like no one understands how you really feel
Explaining doesn't seem to be worth the trouble anymore
No one seems to be listening
You don't want to burden anyone with your life
So you endure without reaching out to friends
Who knows maybe they too are experiencing the same struggles
You are in a place where darkness rules
Finding hope seems damn near impossible
All you want is for your life to turn around and find some peace
Everything is such a struggle these days
You don't mind struggling if you could see tangible results
But you find yourself in the same place you were as before
It's getting harder and harder to wake up every morning
Still believing that today everything will change
That today your ship will finally come in
But what choice do you have?
Giving up is not an option it's not how you were raised
So you do what millions of others do every single day without complaint
You put your head down, go to work and pay your bills
You continue to believe in a dream that was once so close
You just don't know if you have what it takes anymore.

6.28.15...1:03 pm
Listening to Alone Again (Naturally) by Gilbert O'Sullivan

Grace

In times of adversity we cling to what gives us strength
We dig down deep to find the grace of forgiveness
It is a well that might be empty but replenished by the grace of God
For those who have done us wrong we try not to judge them
Instead we pray for their souls lost in the darkness of hate and prejudice
Through the power of prayer may the light of the Lord illuminate
their hearts
May they one day come to understand the grief they have caused
We ask that God give us wisdom to understand what is seeminglyso
incomprehensible
Such beauty forever extinguished
Memories give us solace when we are inconsolable
God has a bigger plan than any of us can ever see
Though sometimes it's hard to walk blindly by faith
And yet we walk because we believe
That in the end of all of this will make sense to us
We continue to live and breathe through God's grace.

6.29.15...9:50 at work
Listening to Cat's in The Cradle by Harry Chapin

Stay Still

The command is not in his words but the tone of his voice
It makes me weak and scatters my thoughts
I ache to feel his hands on my skin
To wrap him tightly inside the warmth of my love
So I can close my eyes and exhale this heat that is driving me crazy
His breath in my ear starts the countdown to pleasure
Soon I won't be able to control myself any longer
Again he murmurs the words in my ear....*stay still*
I crave the punishment of being disobedient
My body refuses to listen, just this once.

6.30.15...8:52 am on the train
Listening to With or Without You by U2

Shiver

A memory makes me shiver for your touch
You have this way of staring deep into my soul
It leaves me feeling naked and vulnerable
I want to confess sins that are not even mine
I want to tell you secrets no one has ever heard
I want you to talk shit to me that makes me blush
Then at the cusp of my arousal, kiss me without permission
Take me to that place where reality feels likes fiction because it feels
so damn good
There are no stop signs on my body
You have the green light to proceed without caution
There are things a woman wants done and she should not have to ask
You send shivers through my body
Then you kiss my soul to calm the disturbance.

7.1.15...8:15 on the train
Listening to I Feel Good All Over by Stephanie Mills

Full

You have no idea what you do to me
It's the most unbelievable feeling I have ever felt
I did not know I was capable of being so overwhelmed
That my mind could be so aroused
That my body could be so hungry
I feel like a virgin all over again
Even though I am a grown woman and given birth to children
You remind me of things I once wanted before life took over
You make me smile so hard my face hurts
You make me ache so much sometimes I cry when I am alone
When I finally see you again my emotions take over
The only way to explain it is to say I feel full with love
It's all because of you I have discovered myself
You have awakened the woman I always knew I could be.

7.3.15...11:09 outside in the yard having some coffee
Listening to Show and Tell by Al Wilson

Whisper Softly

Whisper softly to my heart
Words meant for only me to hear
Tell me some of your secrets
The ones you have been too scared to share
Your burden doesn't have to be so heavy
My shoulders are strong don't let my gender fool you
Behind these closed doors you can put your armor down
There are no battles here to be fought
Your honor is not at stake
Let me into your thoughts even the darkest places
I want to see that side of you that you desperately try to hide
We have come together this far and I am not going anywhere
I am here for the long haul, the good and the bad
I just need you to let me in because silence doesn't protect
It only drives a wedge between lovers
It creates doubt when we should be getting closer
The only way to keep us strong is to discuss our problems
Work together on finding a solution
A relationship only survives when we are in it together.

7.3.15...1:26 in the afternoon
Listening to Sweet Child O' Mine by Guns N' Roses

The Best Woman

Even though we didn't have our forever
I want you to know you are the best woman I have everknown
I was too young to appreciate the strength behind your beauty
I misunderstood it as a challenge to mymanhood
Being a woman doesn't mean being submissive without an opinion
It's only now I see you were trying to lift me up
You were challenging my views but you were always respectful
The little boy in me would rage in anger
The man I am now would communicate better
You were teaching me lessons in love I wasn't ready to learn
What I thought a man should be drove us apart
My pride kept me from apologizing
If I knew better I would've gotten on my knees
Asked for your hand in marriage
I would have done so many things differently
The irony is you laid the foundation for who I am today
Another woman is now reaping the rewards of your hard work
Another man is now loving you the way I didn't know how to then
Beneath the smile and casual hello when we are with our significant other
Lives regret of a life unexplored
We could have been great together and now, we will never ever know.

7.4.15...10:49 am
Listening to So Amazing by Luther Vandross

You

You warm my soul when I need someone to believe in
You lead me out of the darkness without me ever asking
You find the smile in my frown to get me to tomorrow
You hold my hand and we sit in silence
You have been a friend by simply showing up
No grand gestures or big promises of making it all better
You do the hard work necessary of what it means to be a friend
You say you don't want my thanks or even my gratitude
All you expect of me is to keep on trying without making any excuses
Any less from me would be disappointing
I never want to disappoint you
I will keep on fighting because you believe in me
You see something in me I just don't see in myself
But maybe with each day that passes and my confidence grows
I will one day look in the mirror and see the treasure you say I am.

7.6.15...1:15 in the morning
Listening to The Ragged Sea by AlexiMurdoch

Silence

In the silence of my thoughts
I am in bed naked by myself
I can feel your breathe on my skin
Your body pressed against my bosom
Our hearts are beating in unison
You whisper in my ears and I blush
You rise in pursuit of my pleasure
The flower in my garden is blooming
Our voices form a duet in exhalation
You are the bass and I am the falsetto
We make love and beautiful music is created
You are a love song I can never tire of
You are the one I have been waiting for all my life.

7.8.15...6:38 waiting for the bus
Listening to We're In This Love Together by Al Jarreau

Life Happens

I feel lost these days
Not in that special way I once did when I was a teenager
When my imagination allowed me to escape into a world of make believe
It is the kind of lost where you don't know who you are anymore
It's that crushing feeling that somehow the world has passed you by
Who you were supposed to be has given up to find another life
The person staring back in the mirror is a stranger
You wonder how did you get to be this age
It seems as if one day you were carefree, and then the next, life just
happened
You want to ask the questions how did it come to this
But the answers would scare you more than comfort your thoughts
Everyone you know seems to be happy but you know better now
Beneath the smiles and busy schedules they too feel as if something is amiss
You cannot quite put your finger on the discontent
Life was supposed to be much more than this
But somewhere along the line things changed
Monotony became acceptable
Dreams were slowly being forgotten
You allowed yourself to slip through the cracks
What you found is not the life you envisioned
The road to personal redemption isn't lined with gold
You are not entitled to things as you once believed
Getting to the top of the mountain will take hard work
Mediocrity requires nothing at all
Talent is not enough to separate you from the crowd
The sooner you realize this truth the better off you will be
Feeling lost is never an excuse not to keep trying
It is a rite of passage into being an adult
Not everything will be handed to you on a silver platter
Pick yourself up find that well of reserve strength
Go find the life that you know you were meant to live.

7.10.15…10:47 in the morning at work
Listening to Don't Stop by FleetwoodMac

Sleeper

One last look at you before sleep claims us for the evening
Who knows if morning will kiss us awake for one more day
If you are the last face I ever see then I am okay with that image
Nothing in this life is ever promised
So treat each day as God's blessing
In a few minutes your eyes will flutter close
You are already dreaming of something beautiful
Our bodies come together seeking warmth and the comfort of love
Funny how having someone next to you makes you feel safe
My fingertips glide slowly across your naked body
You murmur at the sensation of being touched
I kiss your shoulders ever so slightly
You have always been such a light sleeper
The night is ready to retire for the evening
I whisper in your ear and my words fill your heart
My arms close around you and we fall asleep together
Maybe for one last time

7.13.15...8:20 am
Listening to Crash Into Me by Dave Matthews

Your Lips

Those lips of yours I must confess
Are the softest I have ever felt in my life
When they touch my skin and I close my eyes
It feels like I am floating on a cloud and about to faint
It is the most incredible, sensual feeling that keeps me smiling
I am impatient until the next time we kiss
Butterflies are flying and spinning in my stomach
Sometimes I get so damn nervous
Anticipating softly biting your bottom lip again
Kissing sensually is like reading beautiful poetry
It would be too much for a fragile heart to take
Every kiss is felt and the music of the heart is stirred
A kiss opens the door to your heart
Sometimes love follows in its path
Awakening the yearnings to stimulate your thoughts
This magic happens because our lips had an intimate conversation.

7.13.15...12:06 pm
Listening Ganja Farmer by Marlon Asker

Serena

When what was created naturally is no longer valued
When the standard of beauty does not fit a certain description
Everything else is viewed as less than to sell a narrative
The challenge becomes being inclusive
Beauty by definition is subjective
Viewed through a prism of an already narrow focus
Anything else that doesn't fit the societal norm is met with indifference
New terminology to create separate but equal, like not classically
beautiful becomes in fashion
The not so subtle undermining of a culture continues to persist
The femininity of our women is always being called into question
As if our beauty is some dark forbidden mystery
As if Webster's definition is meant for only one race
What is this need to constantly try and tear us down?
A futile attempt to keep us in our place
Our place is anywhere we want to be
We are just as beautiful as you, no less or no more
There is a rainbow of beauty to discover beyond your own
Open your prism of supposed beauty superiority and recognize that
black is beautiful too.

7.13.15...6:38 pm
Vibing from anger as I channel my thoughts into (aces) as I ride the Blue Line.
Listening to Cranes by Solange

Deserve

What we deserve we don't always get in this life
As a woman you deserve a man who will not take you for granted
Your opinions should always be valued and respected
A law should not have to be passed to make you equal
You should not require the approval of a man to be who you are
That sort of thinking should be outdated but today it is still flourishing
The things you deserve cannot be found in someone else
You cannot wait for someone to validate your existence
You have to lead by example
Leaders cannot change minds by being followers
The world remains the same if everyone is in agreement
You must carve your own lane
Follow your own direction
Be true to the spirit of who you are
Settling for less than you are worth is a recipe for disaster
It will always leave you wanting and wondering
The things you deserve are within your grasp
You just have to believe you have what it takes
Don't allow anyone or anything to stand in your way.

8.1.15...10:17 am. Listening to Daniel by Elton John

Not Good Enough

Maybe I should not feel this way
But after all the hurt I have suffered in my life
After being constantly disrespected without cause
After giving everything I have to the ones I love
Maybe I am not meant to be loved
Maybe I am just not good enough
There must be something about me
Maybe a defect in my personality
No one can seem to see the good person that I am
All they want to do is take from me without ever giving
My kindness is victimized
While evil is rewarded with riches
I am tired of looking for the good in people
I am tired of turning the other cheek and being a good Christian
I have done my best to follow the Bible
To heed the word of my Lord and savior, Jesus Christ
I will not say he has forsaken me
Even though it feels sometimes I am living in the shadows
While his love is shining its light on everyone else
I feel forgotten
I feel invisible
I feel that my life doesn't matter to anyone
They don't see me as a person
But more as a servant without needs and feelings
Maybe they will miss me when I am gone
Maybe then my absence will finally be noticed.

7.25.15...1:23pm
Listening to Say Goodbye by Dave Matthews Band

You Love Me

You have this way of staring at me
My breath gets caught in my throat
It leaves me naked without any answers
It is as if your heart is asking me a silent question
I answer with kisses filled with passion
A hunger for you emanates from deep within my soul
I am only nourished when I feel your touch
My kisses become more urgent
My need for you leaves me vulnerable
You are still hungry for something deeper
Something that keeps eluding your grasp through the years
I want to give you what you need, but I fear it is not enough
I want to sweep you away from everything you know
A place where our past doesn't matter
A place where we can start all over
Let love flourish at its own pace without the nuisance of expectations
The moments we spend together are fleeting
Each one more precious than the next
I look forward to being in your presence where I can be myself
I can exhale and forget the world for a few hours
Your arms are my sanctuary
Your smile fills me with hope of better things to come
Even though you have not said the words as yet
I am hopeful that you see me in your future
There are many things I want us to share together
So many experiences I have never known
Even though you haven't said the words as yet
I know you feel them and for now that is enough.

8.1.15...9:55 am on a beautiful Saturday morning.
Listening to Cause I Love You by Lenny Williams

Sweet Soca

Last night I slept inside your Caribbean warmth
You shuddered a few times then drifted off to sleep
The scent of rain perfumed our bedroom
The sheets were cool against our naked skin
Raindrops danced Soca on the galvanize roof
Pelted the louvers with frenetic sweat
Birds serenaded nature outside the window when we woke up
We listened to all these sounds like a captive audience
The sweetest Soca was listening to you singing in joyful pleasure
Your voice dripping like the juices of a Julie mango
I tasted its flavor and swallowed its nectar
I remained still, immovable, for fear of disturbing the moment
Listening quietly as your voice slowly drifted to barely a whisper.

8.2.15...12:24 pm
Listening to Don't Rock It So by Baron

Just For Him

Come here he says to me in that voice
A voice that instantly stirs the fire within
Making me forget who I am
Transforming me into who I want to be just for him
Just for him I would forget my principles
Just for him I would leave myself vulnerable knowing my heart could
be broken
The path to my sanity would be closed forever
Just for him I am willing to take that chance again
It's a gamble on my future even though my past has taught me better
Just for him,
I will take that walk to the edge of insanity one more time
Hoping when I look down he will be there to catch me when I fall
Just for him I would do anything without ever needing a reason
Simply because to deny him is just not in my nature.

8.18.15...7:59 pm
Slip Slidin' Away by Paul Simon

Something Special

You never have to ask to feel my lips on yours
They are yours to enjoy whenever you want
I kiss you even when you are not around
It comforts me to know our connection goes so deep
It sends currents of electricity surging through my body
Imagining you sucking on my tongue
Your hands caressing my face
Your lips insistent on having their way
Imagining you doing things to me makes me weak
Kissing you is like making love, slow, deep and always sensual
It leaves me with a sense of hope for the future
A hope until you I have never felt before
Even if that hope is false and based in my imagination
It makes me smile in an otherwise uneventful day
Knowing my heart can be touched after so much sadness
You have given me a gift that cannot be bought
No matter what happens between us
I will always be grateful that we shared something special.

7.25.15...8:05 pm
Listening to If Ever You're In My Arms Again by Peabo Bryson

A Mother Knows

A mother knows her daughter
As intimately as she knows herself
No words are needed to convey her heart
It still beats inside of her even after birth
A mother knows when her child is in love or in the midst of pain
It is that sixth sense that mothers have
A bond that's never severed and remains intact
A mother knows her daughter because she is a younger version of herself
A mirror into the mystery of who they are.

8.30.15...12:11am
Listening to Wind Beneath My Wings by Bette Midler

The Beautiful Struggle

Your spirit is beautiful and free
Don't ever let anyone tell you how high you can fly
Don't ever let tell them you the things you can and cannot do
The world in all its beauty can be an ugly place
It can shatter your dreams before they are even born
Human beings are the purveyors of the greatest destruction
You cannot succumb to the limits society places upon your imagination
You must by any means necessary find your voice, the truth of your
convictions
You have been silent for far too long
It is time you screamed for the world to hear
You have things to say of great importance
Others will listen as you awaken their thoughts
They too have been sleeping and something you say will arouse their mind
You are far more powerful than you can ever imagine
Even if you only touch just one person
It is one less lost soul in the world
In your spirit you carry the history of a people who refuse to be forgotten
You are the vessel charged with telling their stories
No matter how painful, truth owes you nothing except to be told
Stand firm, do not waver, even when the truth is met with indifference
You are feeding your spirit needed nourishment the world cannot supply
It begins with your own beautiful struggle to define your life
You are an empty vessel as you make your way through the world
It is up to you to fill it with memories, experiences, travels, regrets and
most of all purpose
The beautiful struggle does not end with you
It has been brewing feeding the souls of our people
The pot keeps stirring long after you are gone
Everything you put into it makes it richer
Your special ingredient enhances the flavor
It enhances the struggle of those who will come after
Someone will eat and be filled because your beautiful struggle
nourished their spirit.

*10.5.15...5:34 on the train. Written after reading Between The World And Me
by Ta-Nehisi Coates. Listening to #41 by Dave Matthews Band*

Soul Energy

A whirlwind of emotions swirl inside my being
A volcano of feelings is about to suddenly erupt
There is no safety net to save me from myself
This is how I get whenever you come around
Everything is heightened
The air crackles with nervous energy
I become this other person
I am under the influence of your aura
One taste of your loving and I become addicted
One more kiss and I will speak the words on my heart
I don't want to be cured of this ailment
It is euphoric losing control of your senses
Not knowing what will happen next no longer makes me anxious
I am caught up in this hurricane of tsunami emotions
I want to be tossed to and fro
I want to be engulfed in a sea of unpredictability
I am tired of playing it safe when it comes to love
I want to fly free without a safety net
The ground is hurtling towards me as I free fall through space
Maybe you will save me this time
Maybe love will let me down again
Whatever happens from this moment on I won't feel regret
This is life in all its beauty and heartbreak
Sometimes you have to take the leap to reap the rewards
This soul energy is nourishing my spirit
I will live in the moment and don't worry about what happens next.

11-10.15...9:15 in the morning...Late In the Evening by Paul Simon

Clouds

So many times I wanted to tell you I loved you but I know it's too late now
The sun has already set on us and it's filled with gray clouds
Someone else beat me to the punch, even though I was there first
The words were always on the tip of my tongue
And we weren't even making love
Saying the words would create too many expectations or so I thought
I didn't want to let you down so I kept my feelings to myself
When you would say you love me for no reason at all
The look in your eyes said you spoke from your heart
Even though I never said those three words back to you
When you turned around I would mouth them silently on my lips
Hoping you could feel my heart without me having to say the words
Wishing your body was a mirror so you could see the reflection of my
feelings
That's always the coward's way out but at least you would know you
were loved
You meant more to me than I have ever shown
It's a confusing thing to feel both sad and happy now
Sadness that you are no longer part of my life
Sadness that all the beautiful things we shared now only live in my memory
I am happy that someone is loving you in the way I never could
Love should never hide in the darkness, it needs to grow in the light
of freedom
It needs to bloom into its full beauty without restrictions
You deserved more than I ever gave you and not because I didn't want to
At some point, I just didn't know how to anymore
It's hard to love someone else when you don't even love yourself
So as the clouds set on what we once shared
I am thankful for at least having a moment in the sun to bask in your aura
I am thankful that you saw something in me to love
And I hope when enough time has passed between us
You will mostly remember me fondly
Maybe smile at a long forgotten memory and then smile at the one
who loves you now.

Listening to Bitter Sweet Symphony by The Verve
11-11.15...11:05 in the morning

Something So Beautiful

In the melancholy of my thoughts and dreams
It's the only place we now talk
I can still hear your voice, taste your passion
Feel the warmth of your skin against mine
We would make love for hours then talk about everything
Kissing and laughing a natural extension of our affection
The sound of your laughter resonating, awakening my heart
You would look at me so intensely, no words were needed
We were something special never to fully bloom
What could have been was aborted
I clumsily cast you aside, not in malice
But a belief that you deserved better than I could offer
I loved you that much, even though I never said the words
You never knew it raged in my soul for you
Even now, months later, no communication
I follow your digital footprints
When I allow myself to feel the pain of losing you
It pierces me as just deeply
Bringing me to tears that won't stop flowing
I hear your laughter just as clearly
I feel your lips just as softly on mine
I can hear you saying my name
How I loved how your voice, so sensual and soft caressed every syllable
How many times have I dialed your number but lost heart
How many times I have written you emails and texts and erased them
Maybe it's a combination of pride, loneliness, letting you go
None of it works anymore to stop this bleeding
A self-inflicted wound not even time can heal
My heart has been broken before but this is different
It's like life suddenly ending for no reason
It's like a song ending somewhere in the middle
Or like a story missing the final chapter
You are left with a feeling, wondering what the hell just happened.

9.12.17 Listening to Adorn by Miguel.

Eternity

Even after all these years
My stomach gets tied up in knots
My thoughts are racing a thousand miles a minute
So excited and nervous I get to be in your arms
To see that smirk on your face
Telling me you're happy to see me again
As you kiss the lipstick on my lips
For your pleasure I wear the red dress you love
Fingers and toes painted for your delight
A special surprise just for your eyes
I blush to myself and laugh out loud in the car
The things you do to me are so amazing
This is what love feels like
So overwhelmed I want to pull over to catch my breath
But one more minute without you is an eternity
Foot heavy on the gas I make haste to see the man I love.

9.14.17
Stir It Up by Bob Marley

Freedom

Love me like this she said, slow and deliberate
Take your time slow the moment down
We have the entire day ahead of us to make love
Kiss me slow and tender,
Find those soft places to make me blush
Whisper sexy words in my ears to make me smile
Let the sun warm my skin
Let your lips set fire to my soul
Let us just exist in the moment
Consume me with an inferno of love
The kind filled with passion to rain tears from my eyes
There is magic in your love, the way you touch me
It is as if your hands are under my skin
Releasing my inhibitions and all my fears
You allow me to be free
A freedom I wasn't aware I needed
You gave me permission to be unashamed
To embrace my sexuality wherever it leads
It is a gift that can never be repaid

9.15.17
Waiting In Vain by Bob Marley

Sleepless

There are nights when the burden of loneliness suffocates
Breathing becomes unbearably painful
The emptiness becomes a shield against the world
I want to die without you here naked in my arms
But dying would stop me from dreaming of your smile
Death is too permanent if a second chance is allowed
Only your touch can make me exhale
But it is mine no more to feel its warmth of love
It is mine now only in sleepless nights of memories
Sometimes when I allow myself to remember us
The pain is at once unbearable and beautiful
So much love could exist between two people
Even now, I feel it drowning my soul
Crossing over boundaries and defenses to keep you at bay
Here you still are,
Here I still am.

Listening to Something Beautiful by Alexi Murdoch
10.11.17…4:21 pm

Moments

The days are winding down
Hours are becoming shorter
There is a quiet urgency now embraced
The final days are not here yet
But they are charging hard across the horizon
Moments once taken for granted
Have a bittersweet taste of melancholy
Unspoken thoughts are in every action
Not a minute should be wasted
Summer's heat reminds you of your first love
Winter's touch reminds me of a broken heart
Spring gives hope that all is not lost
Love should never be taken for granted
She may never come around again
Her touch will be nothing but a memory
Forever living in your heart.

10.11.17…7:15 pm
Listening to Old Man by Neil Young

Tremors

Kisses so soft
Tremors course through my body
Leaving me shivering in the warmth of desire
Stealing my breath for a moment
Igniting a fire in my soul
You give me life
When you are gone, I am lost, my fire dims
Please don't ever leave again
What you provide me is irreplaceable
I don't know where I am
I just know I am safe when you are here
My heart rate elevates
My face flushed with arousal and hunger
Words go silent on my tongue
My body is waiting for your command
I allow my eyes, my touch, to communicate my feelings
Letting you know how overwhelmed I am again
My words would betray my feelings,
Even if you already know how deeply you are loved
This place where only your love can take me is our private haven
A sanctuary I don't want to share with anyone else but you
Tremors are still alive in my body
You kiss me again and life once again makes sense.

Listening to The Secret Garden by Quincy Jones
11.29.17…11:44 am

Jealousy

My mind is going crazy wondering what you are doing
Texts from hours ago have gone unanswered
This is how being on the other side of love feels like
Irrational thoughts fill my mind with darkness
Jealousy takes me down a path which can only be destructive
Images of another touching you in intimate places
Someone is making you laugh and cry from joy and passion
These are things that once belonged to me
I am spiraling out of control
You are not here to save me from myself
Maybe my phone isn't working
Maybe my carrier has cut off my service
And then, just like that you reappear on my screen
Just as you never ever left me
You fell asleep for a few hours and you apologize
You will never know the anguish I felt in those moments
Jealous rage consumed me like a hurricane
This is how you felt for so many years
I still don't understand why you never left.

1.16.18...2:16 PM
Listening to Goodbye Stranger by Supertramp

I'm Not Ready

My body is physically ready to receive your love
It has been far too long since we connected
But my heart remains fragile on the verge of breaking
I am scared of falling into that place again
This time I won't be able to recover from the fall
Who will be there to soothe my heart
Who will be there to wipe my tears
When you are elsewhere loving someone else
I am here all alone in a bed which still holds your scent
Shadows of us dancing on the walls
My body still feels your touch
Your words of love I can still hear being whispered in my ears
You are all around me, and yet, you are not here
I am not ready to lose myself to love again
Only to find myself all alone when evening comes.

12.5.17...2:06 PM
Listening to You're So Vain by Carly Simon

Urgency

There is this sudden fierce urgency I cannot explain
As if an unknown force is speaking to my heart
In a voice I have heard before saying nothing is guaranteed
It hurts me to know someone else is in my space
Someone else is loving you in my absence
An absence created by my selfishness
My thoughts are going crazy, wondering
Are you creating memories making me a memory, a thing of the past
Will the day come when you think of us with fleeting regret
What once was filled with potential is now buried
What we meant to each other has ebbed with time
The breath of life is short
Urging me to make amends and speak my peace before it's too late
Tell her you love her before there is no more time
She needs to hear it from your mouth, face to face
She needs to know she matters to you beyond the physical
She needs to know when you make love, that she is loved
It is not merely a gesture of words, an act of kindness
Love deserves to know it is embraced
Love deserves to know it has grown roots
Love needs to know it is not taken for granted
When you have spoken the words, it is only then the journey begins
An uncertain path is assured
It is clearer now when you know you are seen
Love in all its beauty and complexities should never be invisible
It should be seen as clearly as a brand new day.

Listening to I Am a Rock by Paul Simon
1.10.18…9:34 AM

Promises

There are promises I want to make but cannot keep
Words I want to whisper to your heart so it can soar
I want to make the little girl inside smile again
And whisper in her ears she will never be second
There are so many thoughts I wish to share
But our time is always so limited
We are never free to fully exhale and enjoy the moment
The shadow of time always casting its doubt
The night staring at us with her furrowed brows
Your once soft edges hardened by mistrust
Your smile once sunny is cloudy
Beneath the surface you are still there
Not hiding but being cautious
A heart can only hurt so many times
Eyes can only cry so many tears
You have to protect yourself
Even from those who claim to have your best interest
When heartbreak comes only you can carry its burden
We may never get back to the innocence of love
You trusting me with your heart and all its secrets
As if it were the most natural thing in the world
There are things I say to myself when I am all alone
I only wish I could say them to your face
And let them be more than just words.

1.16.18…2:48 PM
Listening to Crazy Love by Van Morrison

Three Words

I hear you crying early in the morning
It's a daily occurrence now
My eyes are closed as I pretend to be sleeping
I don't have the words of poets to ease your pain
It's a burden I would gladly carry for you my love
You haven't done anything to deserve this news
Not that anyone ever does
Hearing you cry wounds me in a way I won't ever recover from
I am a man of action and used to solving problems
This one has no solution only the hands of God can heal
Only the windows of time can soothe
So I do the only thing that I can for you as your man
I hold you close
Whisper those three words that are a balm for the soul
Tears tremble through your body
Finally you fall asleep but I don't let you go.

1.16.18...10:14 PM
Listening to Time Passages by Al Stewart

You Don't Say My Name Anymore

You don't say my name the way you used toanymore
I cannot tell you how much I miss this simple thing
I would close my eyes and leave the world behind
Your voice was classical music to my ears
It was Spring, the birds and all that jazz
A song I wanted to have on repeat just so only I could hear
That piece of you that belonged only to me
For that moment I wanted to be selfish and not share your love
Your voice was a whisper in my ear
A deep shudder in my soul
That place I could always call home
It made me feel safe and would calm all my fears
You don't say my name anymore
Your voice has gone quiet
You say you still love me but it doesn't feel the same
I wait for its magic but all I hear is silence these days
Funny the things you miss when they are gone
They were a part of you without even knowing
You don't say my name anymore
I wish I would have known
It would be the last time you said it with love.

1.17.18...2:14 am
Listening to Operator by Jim Croce

Black Girl Magic

We walk through this life knowing all eyes are on us
Waiting for us to fail and claim some sort of moral victory
Watching us with a curiosity not born of innocence
But a desire to own us, possess what is not for sale anymore
Our bodies are talked about and whispered behind our backs
Our intellect questioned and not valued as equal
Our hair poked and prodded as if on display for society's amusement
Our men are not always the first to defend us
Yet, we still love them fiercely because it is who we are as Black Women
Even after all these slights to dim our light
We find a way to rise to give life to our Black Girl Magic
It is a magic passed on from generations of Black women
Women enslaved but never bowed
Chained but never broken
Beaten, raped, defiled and left for dead among the living
Their light was hidden but never stolen
Their hopes and dreams they passed down to their children
Endowing us with a strength we can call on when needed
I see my sisters in all walks of life making their way in this world
Some have already walked into their purpose
Others are on the edge of discovering their true beauty
A beauty that emanates from deep roots bled into our souls
Beating fervently in our hearts and coming to life through the physical
But manifesting its light into something spiritually beautiful
A magic you can touch and feel,
Even as it remains free to change and evolve of its own choosing
The physical embodiment of our Black Girl Magic doesn't merely stop
at what society objectifies
Our beauty is subtle, soft, nuanced, in your face, hidden
It is always evolving into something we have already imagined
But it is always there, waiting to be discovered, appreciated as
something uniquely special
Not to be compared against any other women who are beautiful in
their own right
Black Girl Magic was forged from a painful past
Left for dead, buried and reborn
Once held back by chains and closed minds
Never again.
Never again.

We are more than breasts, hips, thighs and other dissected body parts
We are mind, body and spirit deserving of love
We are all links in a chain forged from a common legacy
A legacy that demands we claim what is rightfully ours, nothing more,
and nothing less
We are here.
We will be seen.
Our crowns have already been paid for
We are no longer invisible.

Listening to Black Pearl by Sonny Charles & The Checkmates
6.11.18…3:16 PM.

Also by Dean Jéan-Pierre

The Pussy Whispers
Woman Worship
Woman Worship 2
Woman Worship 3
Moist
Cum For Me
Insatiable (1&2)
Stiff (E-book)
Assume the Position
Aural Sex (CD)
Kiss Me Softly
The Killing Club of Ex-Girlfriends
*Don't F*ck With Eva (E-book)*
Don't Mess With Eva (1&2)
The Randomness of Everything
Crave

www.ingramcontent.com/pod-product-compliance
Lightning Source LLC
LaVergne TN
LVHW041253080426
835510LV00009B/717